IMAGES
of America

BOSTON UNIVERSITY
HOCKEY

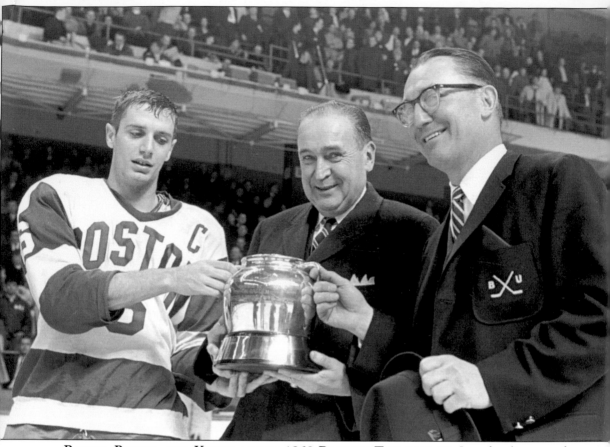

PARKER, POWERS, AND KELLEY AT THE 1968 BEANPOT TOURNAMENT. In a familiar pose for both men, 1968 Terrier captain Jack Parker (6) stands with head coach Jack Kelley (right). The man in the middle is Boston Garden president Eddie Powers. Of all the events hosted by the Garden, the Beanpot Tournament was Powers's favorite. The trophy was renamed for him posthumously in 1974.

IMAGES
of America

BOSTON UNIVERSITY
HOCKEY

Bernard M. Corbett

ARCADIA
PUBLISHING

Published by Arcadia Publishing
Charleston, South Carolina

Printed in the United States of America.

Library of Congress Catalog Card Number: 2002109946

For all general information contact Arcadia Publishing at:
Telephone 843-853-2070
Fax 843-853-0044
E-mail sales@arcadiapublishing.com
For customer service and orders:
Toll-Free 1-888-313-2665

Visit us on the Internet at www.arcadiapublishing.com

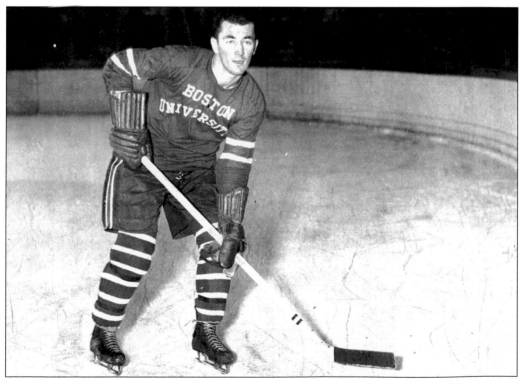

JACK KELLEY '52. As a player, Jack Kelley starred for the Terriers from 1949 to 1952. A top offensive player his sophomore and junior years (49 goals, 26 assists, and 75 points), Kelley switched to the blue line his senior year. He played in two consecutive NCAA tournaments in 1950 and 1951. Kelley is a member of the Boston University Hall of Fame.

CONTENTS

ACKNOWLEDGMENTS

Sincere thanks go to Boston University sports information director Ed Carpenter and his assistant Pete Charboneau; Fred Sway and Rick Young at Boston University photo services; and Sean Pickett, who has independently compiled a Boston University Terrier hockey record book.

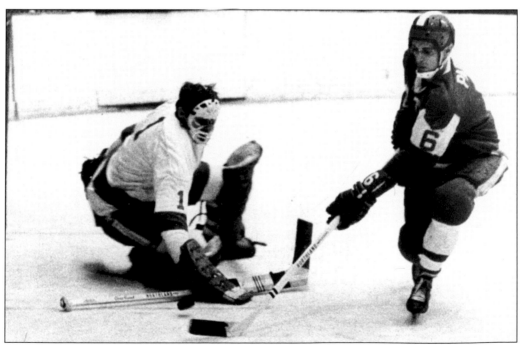

JACK PARKER ON A BREAKAWAY AGAINST GOALIE KEN DRYDEN. Jack Parker (6) was a steady, hardworking center for coach Jack Kelley from 1966 to 1968. Parker also played in two NCAA tournaments in 1966 and 1967, and on three consecutive Beanpot championship teams. Overall, Parker's teams compiled a record of 27-1 versus their Beanpot neighbors. Here, Parker breaks in on legendary Cornell net-minder Ken Dryden. The Terrier-Big Red rivalry was at its peak during the late 1960s and early 1970s. Dryden was named Boston University's most honored opponent of the quarter century by the Friends of Hockey in 1988.

INTRODUCTION

On February 6, 1918, as the Great War to end all wars raged, the Boston University Terriers took to the ice of the Boston Arena for the first time. Their opponent, archrival Boston College, shared the ice with them. Neither school could have known on that fateful night the magnitude and longevity of the war that had begun. The battles now number 211, with the Terriers leading the all-time series with their ancient rivals 108-88-15. Remarkably, with the exception of a season and a half, only four men have directed BU's on-ice fortunes since 1928.

Wayland Vaughn's teams enjoyed consistent success through the 1930s. Forwards Johnny Lax '35 and Paul Rowe '35 were the first in a long line of Terrier players to proudly represent their country and university at the 1936 Olympics in Nazi Germany. Al Carvelli '38 soon followed the estimable exploits of Lax and Rowe on the ice, joining them in the Boston University Hall of Fame. His tenure interrupted by World War II, Vaughn led the Terriers back to formalized competition.

The first of three former players to guide the Terriers to the unprecedented heights of the past half century was Harry Cleverly '37. Cleverly was an outstanding athlete during his scholastic days and brought the Terriers to their first of a record 26 National Collegiate Athletic Association (NCAA) appearances (matched only by Minnesota) in 1950. Led by the prolific offensive contributions of All-American Jack Garrity '51 and the outstanding puck-stopping skills of All-American goalie Ike Bevens '51, the Terriers began to make their mark at the national level.

Cleverly's teams made a total of four national tournament appearances during his final decade as head coach. His 1958 Terriers captured the first of a record 24 Beanpot championships, emblematic of Boston hockey supremacy. The 1959–1960 squad remains one of the school's finest, led by center Bob Marquis '60, a flashy product of Montreal, Quebec, who matched the All-American achievement of Jack Garrity a decade earlier.

In 1962, another prodigal Terrier son returned. Jack Kelley '52, who had been a stellar performer at both forward and defense during his playing days for Cleverly, came back to Commonwealth Avenue from Colby College. Under Kelley's leadership as head coach, the program rose to new heights. A dominant decade included six Beanpot titles, an Eastern Collegiate Athletic Conference (ECAC) crown, and consecutive NCAA championships. The up-tempo, relentless fore-checking style of Kelley's clubs became the Terrier trademark. A total of 11 All-Americans played for Kelley's teams, which compiled a record of 206-80-8.

Jack Parker '68, the team's current head coach, has guided the Terriers since 1973. A captain of Kelley's 1967–1968 team, the native of Somerville, Massachusetts, has become one of college hockey's coaching icons as he nears his third decade at the helm of the Boston University hockey ship. His 655 career wins currently rank him fourth all-time.

At the national level, Parker's Terriers have made 18 national tournament visits, including championships in 1978 and 1995. Regionally, they have won nine ECAC/Hockey East crowns.

Locally, the "Scarlet and White" have simply owned the Beanpot Tournament, claiming the coveted symbol of Boston bragging rights a staggering 17 times.

Parker's players have included center Rick Meagher '77, the school's only three-time All-American; all-time leading scorer John Cullen '87; and a plethora of Olympic and National Hockey League elite performers, including 1998 Hobey Baker Award winner and current Colorado Avalanche star Chris Drury. Perhaps the most recognizable are the "BU Four" (Jim Craig, Mike Eruzione, Jack O'Callahan, and Dave Silk) who played for the 1980 United States Olympic gold medal hockey team.

With a tradition virtually unmatched in the history of the sport of college hockey, this year's Terrier hockey team smoothly skates on, jointing a legendary scarlet-and-white line of excellence.

One

IN THE BEGINNING
(1917–1943)

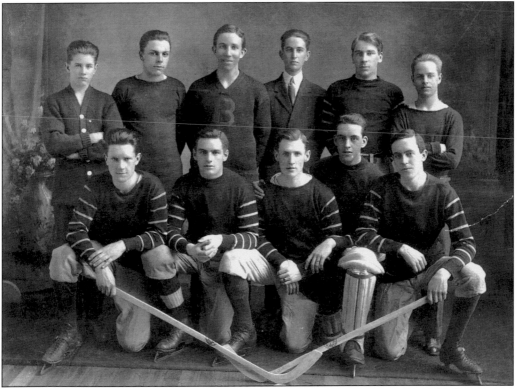

THE FIRST BOSTON UNIVERSITY HOCKEY TEAM (1917–1918). The Terriers made their on-ice debut on February 6, 1918, versus Boston College. A 3-1 loss was followed by an identical result the next year. In both years, it was the only game played by Boston University. The 1919–1920 team lost twice to Boston College and the University of Massachusetts (Amherst). After a two-year absence, the program returned for the 1922–1923 season. Coach John O'Hare became the university's third head coach (following Edgar Burkhardt [1918–1919] and Harold Stuart [1919–1920]), compiling a record of 3-13 from 1922 to 1924. His tenure included the program's first victory, a 6-1 decision over UMass. George Gaw (1924–1928) then took over and led the Terriers to their first two winning seasons (1924–1925 and 1927–1928) and first ever win over Boston College (1-0) in 1924.

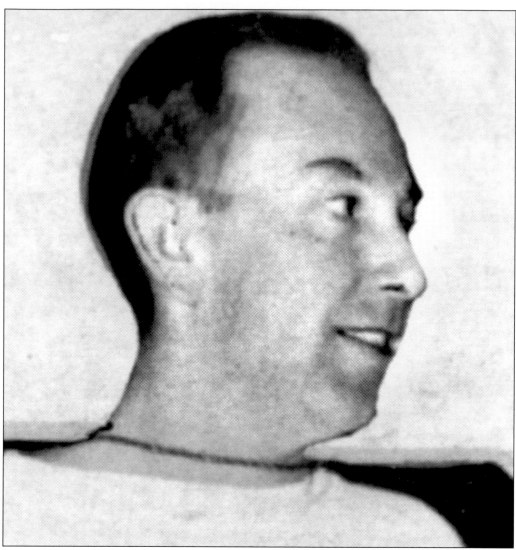

COACH WAYLAND VAUGHN (1928–1940, 1941–1943). Wayland Vaughn became the first of the four Terrier coaches in the 80 years that the program has existed. Vaughn was the first coach to bring the Terriers to prominence in the old New England league. His 9-2 debut season included a pair of wins over Boston College, led by co-captains William Gibson and Sydney Silberberg. Silberberg was the first in the 75-year line of outstanding goaltenders. Overall, Vaughn enjoyed eight winning seasons in his twelve prewar years as head coach. He returned to coach for the two years the Terriers had a formal wartime team (1941–1943). His overall coaching record stands at 86-83-7 for 14 seasons.

JOHNNY LAX '35 AND PAUL ROWE '35.
Johnny Lax (right) was a true pioneer
in establishing Boston University
Hockey as the program of national
prominence it remains today. Lax
was a gifted forward with exceptional
stick-handling and play-making skills,
and combined with fellow legend
Paul Rowe (below) to create one of
the most explosive scoring lines in
school history. The duo co-captained
the 1934–1935 team that rallied to
win five of their last seven games, Lax
and Rowe finishing first and second
in overall scoring. After completing
their playing careers as Terriers, they
were named to the 1936 United
States Olympic team. Competing in
Hitler's Germany, the Terrier tandem
combined for three game-winning
goals as the Americans brought home
a bronze medal. The strong bond
of Boston University and Olympic
hockey was thus forged. Both Lax and
Rowe are Terrier Hall of Famers.

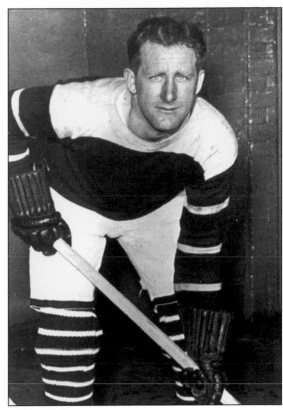

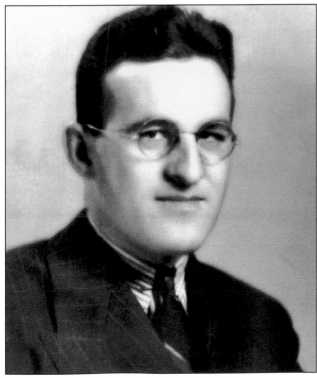

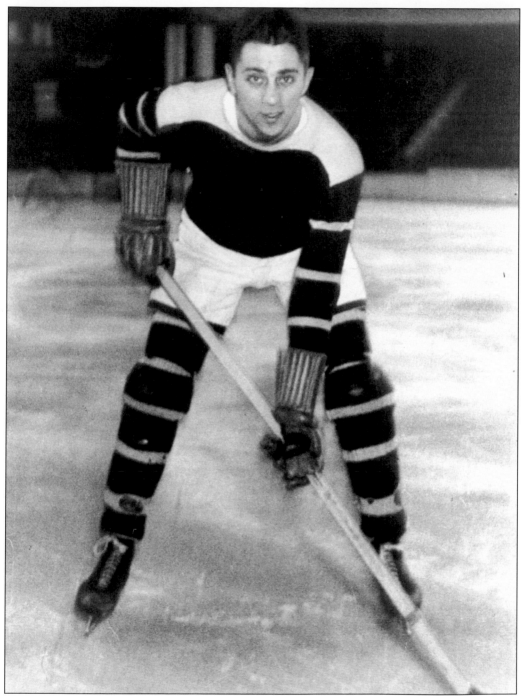

AL CARVELLI '39. The 1938–1939 team was one of coach Wayland Vaughn's best. It was the first Boston University team to hit double figures in wins, with 10. Two victories over Boston College and the program's first ever win over Harvard highlighted the 10-4 campaign. Al Carvelli '39, a future Terrier Hall of Famer, put up prolific scoring numbers. His career totals of 46-38-84 in just 36 games outdistanced all previous Terriers in all offensive categories by a wide margin.

Two
THE CLEVERLY YEARS (1946–1962)

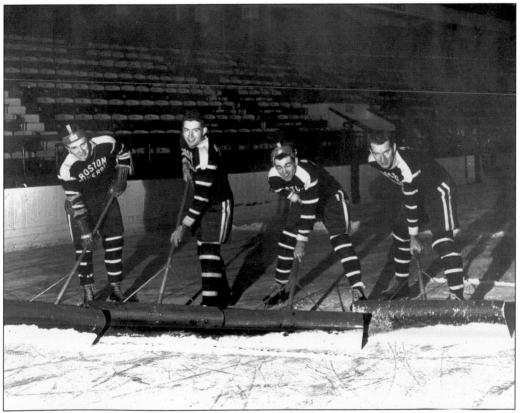

THE 1949 TERRIER "ICE CLEANERS." These four members of the 1948–1949 team show they are not afraid to roll up their sleeves. From left to right are Greater Boston skaters Bob Bell (Framingham), Walter Anderson (Waltham), Don Cleary (Cambridge), and Dick Grant (Arlington). The Terriers "cleaned up" on several opponents that year, compiling an overall record of 13-7 and 7-2 in the New England league.

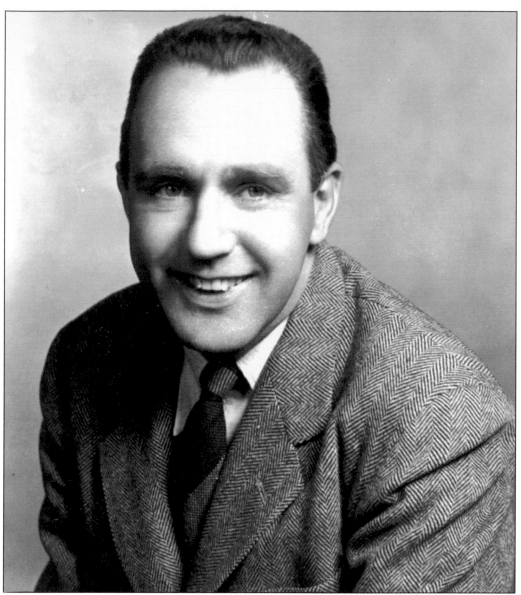

HARRY CLEVERLY '37, HEAD COACH (1945–1962). A letter-winner in hockey, football, and baseball, Harry Cleverly led the Terrier skaters to considerable postwar success. Beginning in 1946, Cleverly's teams strung together seven consecutive winning seasons highlighted by the Terriers' first three NCAA appearances, in 1950, 1951, and 1953. After a two-season sub-.500 slide in the mid 1950s, Cleverly quickly brought the program back to prominence. Notable achievements of the coach's later years included the school's first of a record 26 Beanpot championships in 1958 and a return to the NCAA tournament on the Terriers' home ice at Boston Arena in 1960. Cleverly was the 1958 national coach of the year, and his teams posted an impressive 210-142-10 overall record during his 17-year tenure. Elected to the Terrier Hall of Fame in 1959, Cleverly died tragically in an automobile accident in Vermont on December 3, 1968. A three-sport coach at Boston University, Cleverly also guided the varsity baseball and freshman football squads. The Varsity Club named its annual Coach of the Year award after Cleverly posthumously in 1969.

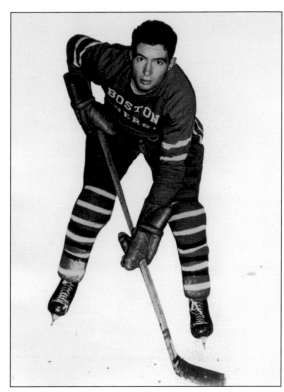

WALTER ANDERSON '50. A three-sport standout in hockey, football, and baseball, Walter Anderson, a native of Waltham, Massachusetts, was the Boston University athlete of the year in 1948. Anderson was named to the inaugural NCAA hockey All-America first team in 1950. During his three varsity seasons, the Terriers combined for a record of 51-16. Anderson was a forward with good offensive skills, and he finished his career with better than a point a game (44 games, 22-27-49). Anderson was also a World War II veteran and saw action in the Pacific. He went on to a coaching career and was elected to the Boston University Hall of Fame in 1961.

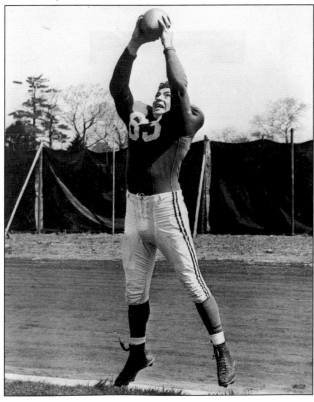

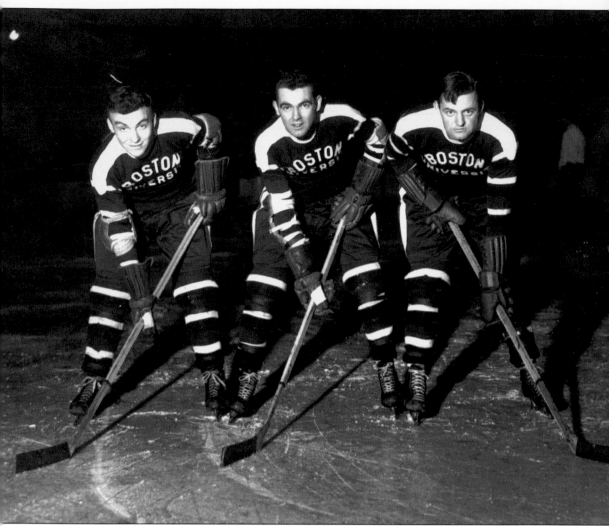

THE 1948 FORWARD LINE: CAPTAIN BEN FORBES, DON CLEARY, AND WILLIAM KIRRANE. The 1947–1948 team was one of Harry Cleverly's finest. A 20-4 record included two 6-5 losses (one in overtime) to a powerful Dartmouth squad. From left to right, the line of captain Ben Forbes (17-13-30), Don Cleary (21-16-37), and William Kirrane (8-13-21) was one of the Terriers' top offensive units.

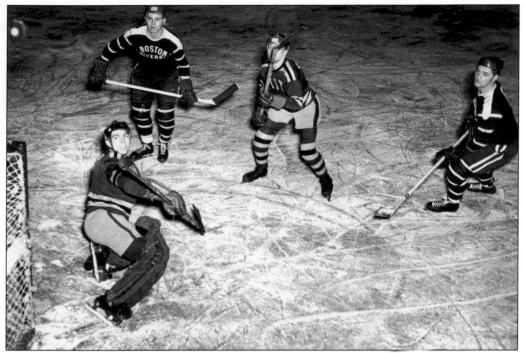

A Melee in Front of the Net. A Massachusetts Institute of Technology goalie comes out of the net in an attempt to stop Boston University's center Ed Cahoon (left) of Melrose, Massachusetts, and William Kirrane (right) of Brookline, Massachusetts. Cahoon's shot missed the cage, but the Terriers came back to post a 10-3 win.

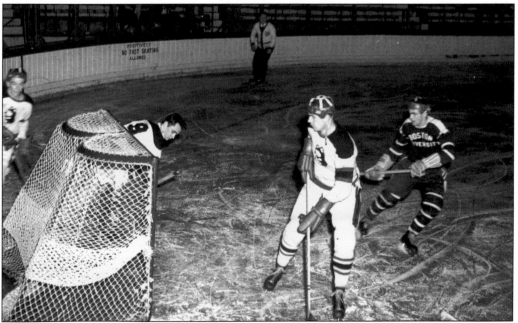

The Terriers Score. Don Cleary (right), a Boston University wing from Cambridge, beats Northeastern University's goalie Bob Howell on a solo rush to put the Terriers in the lead. In front is Husky defenseman Duke Kerriven. The Terriers went on to rack up a 7-4 win.

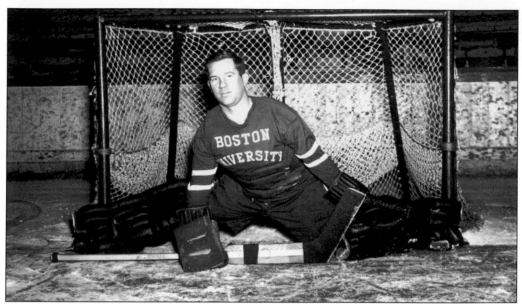

RALPH "IKE" BEVENS '50. Ralph "Ike" Bevens '50 was Boston University's first in a long line of All-American net-minders. Bevens was the captain of the first Terrier NCAA tournament team and backstopped the upset of defending champion University of Michigan in the NCAA semifinals 4-3 at the Broadmoor in Colorado Springs. Despite the Terriers' championship game defeat to Colorado College, Bevens was still named the tournament's Most Valuable Player (MVP). Bevens was a schoolboy standout at hockey power Arlington High School and is a member of the Terrier Hall of Fame.

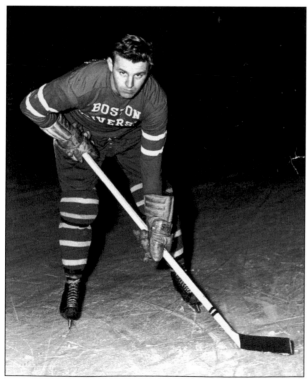

ED CAHOON, CO-CAPTAIN 1950–1951. Ed Cahoon co-captained the 1950–1951 Terriers to a 16-5 season record and a second straight trip to the NCAA tournament in Colorado Springs. Cahoon was a major offensive force in all three of his varsity seasons at Boston University. As a sophomore in 1948–1949, his 25 goals and 40 points led the team. His career numbers (60-58-118) made him one of the first members of the Terriers' 100-point scoring club, along with teammates Jack Garrity '51 and Irv Haynes '50. Cahoon was the longtime head coach at Burlington High School in Massachusetts. The late coach has the distinction of being the last man to lead a Massachusetts public school to a Division I high school state championship.

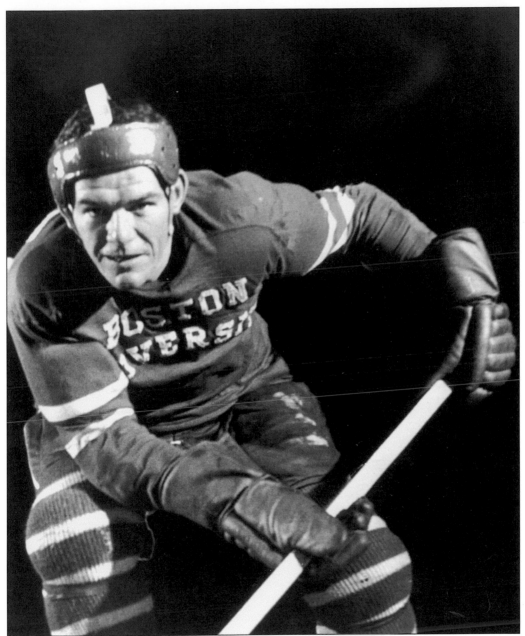

JACK GARRITY '50. Jack Garrity was the defining player in the early years of Harry Cleverly's tenure as Boston University head coach. A member of the 1948 United States Olympic team, Garrity's seasonal marks for goals (51) and points (84) registered during the 1949–1950 season remain Terrier records more than a half century later. His final two seasons as a Terrier, 1949–1950 and 1950–1951, both ended with excursions to Colorado Springs and the NCAA championships. An explosive offensive force from his center ice position, the Medford High School three-sport standout returned from his wartime service and completed his four-year course of study at Boston University in three years, despite being married with two children during his playing days as a Terrier. Garrity is a member of the Boston University Hall of Fame.

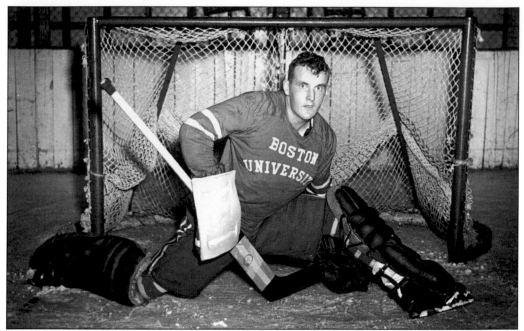

DICK BRADLEY '51. Net-minder Dick Bradley played his first two years in the considerable shadow of All-American Ralph "Ike" Bevens '50. Following Bevens' graduation, Bradley became the number one goalie and promptly led Boston University to a 16-5 record and a return to the NCAA championships at the Broadmoor in Colorado Springs.

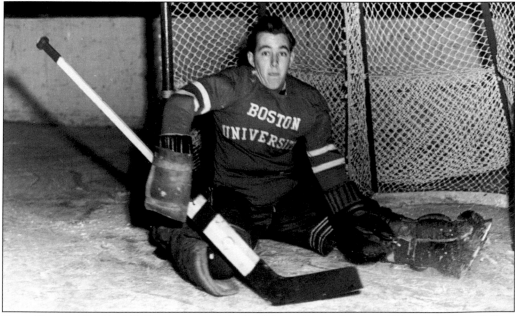

PAUL KELLEY '53. Paul Kelley continued the highly proficient lineage of Terrier goalies. Kelley, as captain, led the 1952–1953 Boston University team back to their third NCAA appearance in four years with a record of 14-7-1. An 11-2 stretch keyed the program's run back to the Broadmoor once again. The late Kelley was teamed with his brother Jack for two of his three varsity seasons.

RICHARD KELLEY '52. The captain of the 1951–1952 Terriers (15-3-1), Richard Kelley finished one point ahead (20-23-43) of Dick Rodenheiser for the team scoring lead. Kelley's career scoring line of 54-66-120 and overall outstanding play earned him induction to the Boston University Hall of Fame.

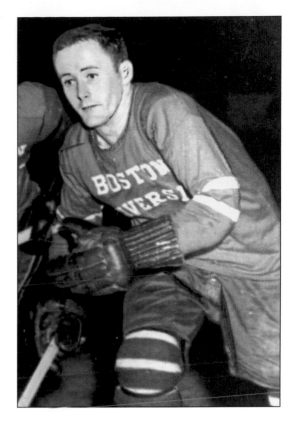

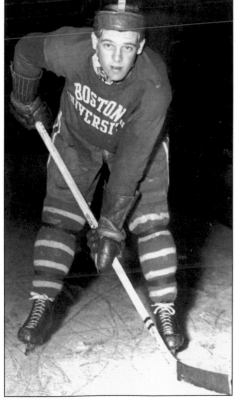

DICK RODENHEISER '53. Dick Rodenheiser led the 1952–1953 NCAA team in all three major offensive categories. His 29-20-49 scoring line was a key element in the Terriers' success. The smallish but swift Malden, Massachusetts, native was the lone Boston University member of the 1960 United States Olympic Gold Medal hockey team. Boston University and the University of Minnesota are the only two schools to place players on both the 1960 and 1980 gold-medal squads. Rodenheiser scored the first-ever goal in the history of the Beanpot tournament versus Northeastern University on December 26, 1952, at the Boston Arena.

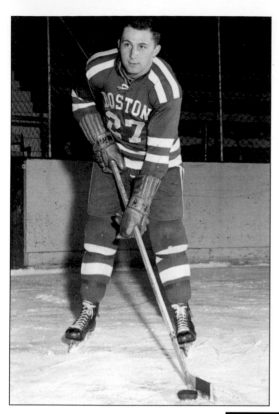

FORBES KEITH '59. Forbes Keith was a consistent offensive performer during his Terrier career. The Brookline, Massachusetts, native scored 67 points (40-27-67) in just 46 games. Keith cracked the 20-goal barrier in his senior year (1958–1959) with 21, finishing second behind Bob Marquis in overall scoring.

LARRY CREIGHTON '59. Forward Larry Creighton co-captained the 1958–1959 team to a 13-8-2 record. Creighton and his fellow co-captain, defenseman Ron DiVincenzo (who went on to become the highly successful coach of the Brookline High School program in Massachusetts), provided solid leadership for a team that put the foundation in place for the team's NCAA run the following season. Creighton narrowly missed the Boston University Century (100-point) Club, with 43-51-94 in 46 career games.

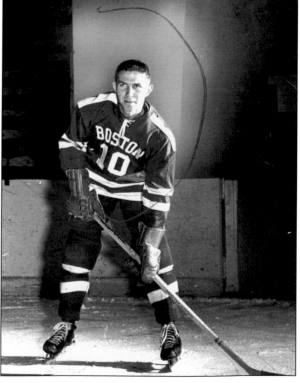

CAPTAIN SARGE KINLIN '58 AND THE 1957–1958 TEAM. Sarge Kinlin co-captained the 1957–1958 team with future Hall of Famer and fellow defenseman Bob Dupuis '58. The 17-5-1 team narrowly missed an NCAA tournament selection, but has the distinction of winning the school's first of 26 Beanpot championships in the tournament's 50-year history. Forward Bill Sullivan was named the tournament's MVP.

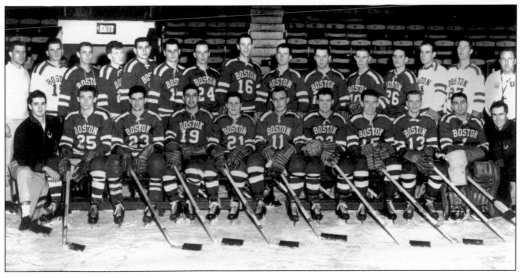

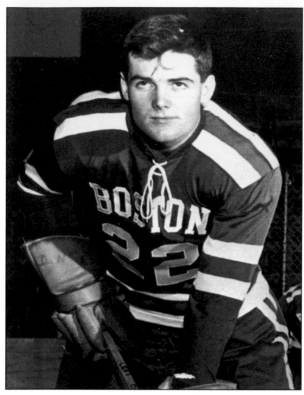

DON MACLEOD '58. Don MacLeod had the distinction of being selected first team All-America in two sports: hockey and baseball. On the ice, Don was a three-time All-East choice as a defenseman and a member of the Terriers' first Beanpot championship team his senior year. MacLeod was the team MVP and university scholar-athlete of the year in 1958 and also enjoyed tremendous success on the diamond, specifically on the mound. A three-year baseball team MVP, Don posted a 17-6 overall pitching record. He went on to pitch four years with the Milwaukee Brewers organization. He is a member of the Boston University Hall of Fame.

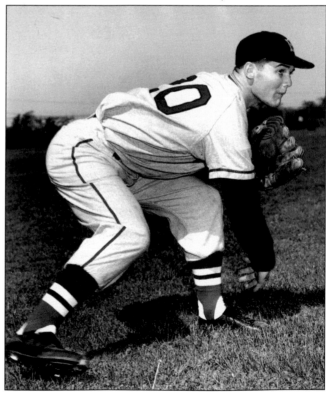

BOB MARQUIS '60. Bob Marquis was the defining player of the later years of Harry Cleverly's tenure as head coach. Marquis was a Montreal area schoolboy with outstanding speed and overall scoring ability. He finished his career owning all three Boston University career scoring marks: goals (98), assists (66), and points (164). He remains the Terriers' all-time leading scorer among three-year varsity players. As co-captain of the 1960 team, Marquis led the Terriers to the NCAA championships on their Boston Arena home ice. A two-time All-American (in his sophomore and junior years), Marquis was not selected in his senior year, which caused considerable controversy. He is a Boston University Hall of Famer.

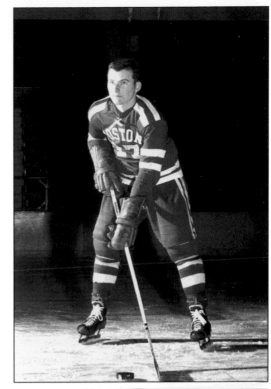

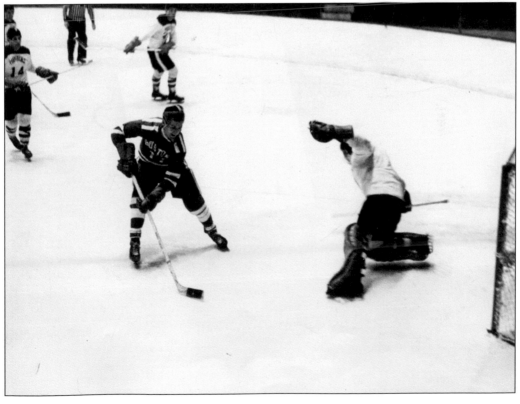

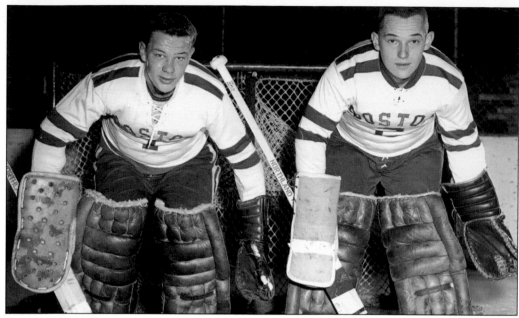

GOALIES GLEN EBERLY '63 AND BARRY URBANSKI '61. From 1959 to 1963, Barry Urbanski (right) and Glen Eberly handled the bulk of the net-minding chores for the Terriers. Urbanski's best season was 1959–1960. As a junior, "the Bear" registered a 12-5 record (3.24 goals against average [GAA] and .907 save percentage), and was selected for the NCAA All-Tournament team. Eberly was the regular goalie for coach Harry Cleverly's last team (1961–1962) and coach Jack Kelley's first (1962–1963). The annual award for the outstanding goalie in the Beanpot Tournament (the Eberly Award) is named after Glen and his brother Dan, a goalie at Northeastern University.

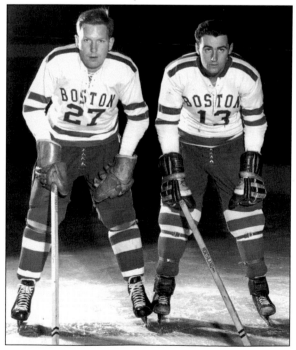

DAVE CARVER '62 AND PETER FITZGERALD '62. Defense partners Dave Carver (left) and Peter Fitzgerald skated together for two years, Harry Cleverly's last two seasons as head coach. The Fitzgerald family endowed a scholarship to honor Peter, a former U.S. Air Force pilot. The award is given annually to the best underclass defenseman. The 2002 recipient was Freddy Meyer.

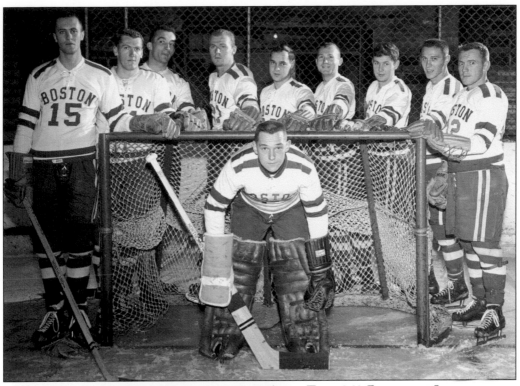

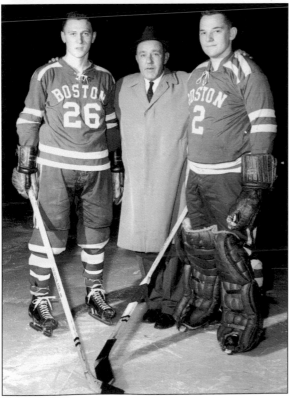

THE 1961 RETURNING LETTERMEN AND CAPTAIN BILL QUINN, COACH HARRY CLEVERLY, AND BARRY URBANSKI. The 1960–1961 returning lettermen (above) fell short of the lofty accomplishments of the previous year. Bill Quinn (left), the second Quinn family member of three to captain the Terriers, led coach Harry Cleverly's penultimate team.

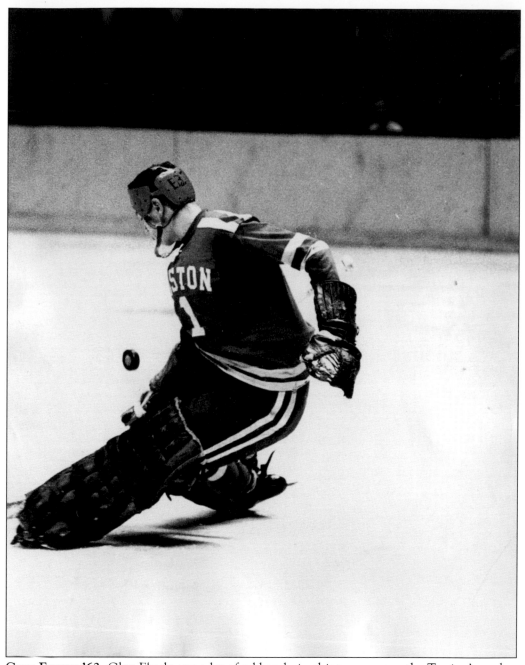

GLEN EBERLY '63. Glen Eberly saw a lot of rubber during his two years as the Terriers' number one goalie. He faced 1,471 shots in 41 games. His career save percentage of .881 is good for 19th on the Terriers' all-time list.

Three

THE KELLEY YEARS (1962–1972)

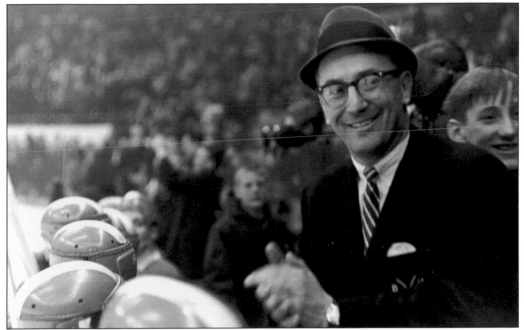

JACK KELLEY '52. Jack Kelley returned to his alma mater a decade after his graduation to become the Terriers' head coach. A highly successful seven years (89-51-5) at Colby College culminated with the college's appearance in the inaugural ECAC tournament at the Boston Garden. In 1962, when Boston University called, Kelley answered with a decade-long run of dominance that catapulted the Terrier program to the pantheon of college hockey locally (six Beanpot titles), regionally (the 1972 ECAC championship) and nationally (four NCAA appearances and two National Championships). Kelley's career record of 206-80-8 on Commonwealth Avenue ranks him among the top college coaches in all-time winning percentage—.714. His last two Terrier teams (1971 and 1972) remain the last in any school to win back-to-back national titles. He left for the pro ranks in 1972. He became coach and general manager of the New England Whalers in the fledgling World Hockey Association (WHA), and his club won the Avco Cup as the league's first champions in 1973. After a 30-year career in professional hockey, Kelley is now retired in Maine (summer) and Florida (winter).

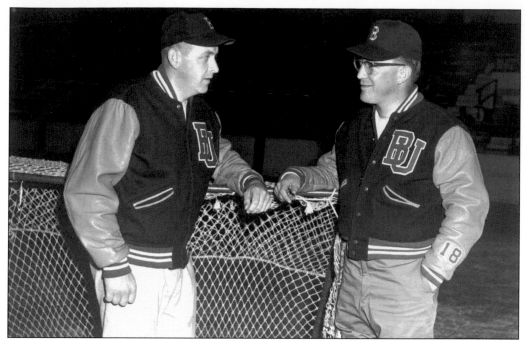

COACH KELLEY WITH ASSISTANT COACH BOB CROCKER. Jack Kelley's alter ego and closest confidant during his decade as Terrier head coach was Bob Crocker (left) '55. As the assistant coach, Crocker's thoroughness and tenacity made him an outstanding recruiter. The Kelley-Crocker coaching team spelled unparalleled success for the Boston University hockey program. Crocker went on to become head coach at the University of Pennsylvania (Penn). He is currently a scout for the New York Rangers and remains a fixture in hockey rinks throughout North America.

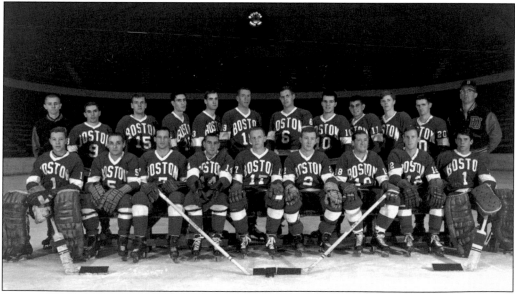

THE 1962–1963 TEAM. Jack Kelley's first Boston University team compiled a record of 8 wins and 16 losses. Mike Denihan (14) was the captain and the team's leading scorer, with 25-14-39.

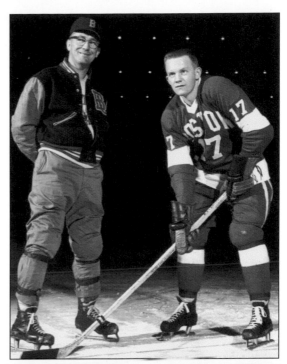

BOB SMITH (17), MIKE DENIHAN (14), AND BOB ROWAN (8). Bob Smith (17) and Mike Denihan (14) were numbers one and two in scoring for both the 1961–1962 and 1962–1963 seasons. In 1961–1962, Smith (also at right with coach Jack Kelley) was the junior captain of Harry Cleverly's last Terrier team, leading Boston University with a record of 19-15-34. Denihan (8-16-24) was the scoring runner-up. Rowan compiled a 9-10-19 scoring line. In 1962–1963, Denihan was captain and scoring leader and Smith finished second in scoring with a record of 13-20-33.

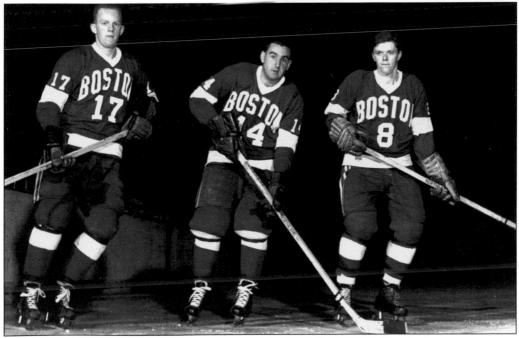

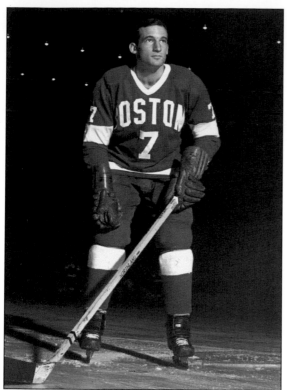

RICHIE GREEN '65. As junior captain of the 1963–1964 Terriers, defenseman Richie Green survived a near tragic accident, breaking his neck in a trampoline accident during a school physical education class. After the incident (lower right) he is shown visiting with coach Jack Kelley (lower left) and goalie Jack Ferreira. Despite the neck injury, Green was still named All-America for his considerable efforts, the only Greater Boston area player so honored. The injury ended the career of the former three-sport schoolboy standout from Watertown, Massachusetts. The defenseman whom National Hockey League (NHL) scouts praised as the "greatest college hockey player" they had ever seen unfortunately never got to take his game to the pros. However, he has been bringing players to the pros as a regular part of his job as a longtime NHL scout for several organizations. Green is a Boston University Hall of Famer.

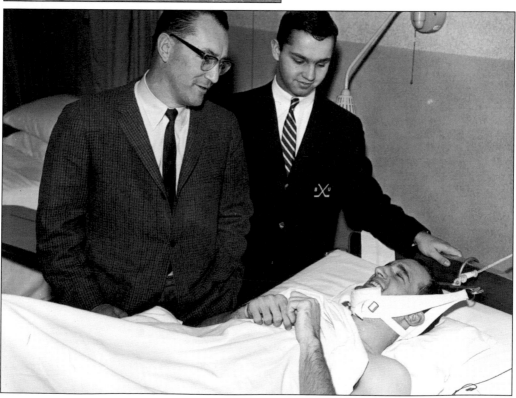

BOB SYLVIA, CO-CAPTAIN 1964–1965.
Jack Kelley's rebuilding project began to
take shape in 1964–1965. Bob Sylvia,
co-captain of the Terrier team with Bob
Martell, led Boston University to a 25-6
record and an appearance in the Beanpot
Tournament final and ECAC semifinals.
Sylvia was second on the team in scoring,
with a record of 17-21-38, and Martell was
fourth (16-19-35).

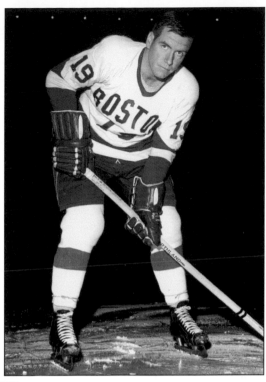

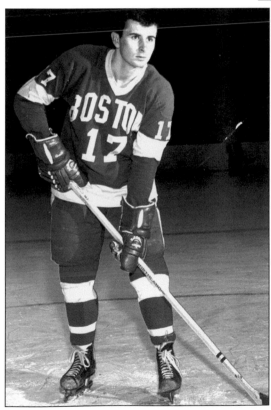

BRUCE FENNIE '66. Bruce Fennie
was a top Terrier sniper for three
seasons. As a junior, he led the team
in scoring with 21-21-42. Bruce
improved his senior year to 23-30-53
and finished second to Fred Bassi.

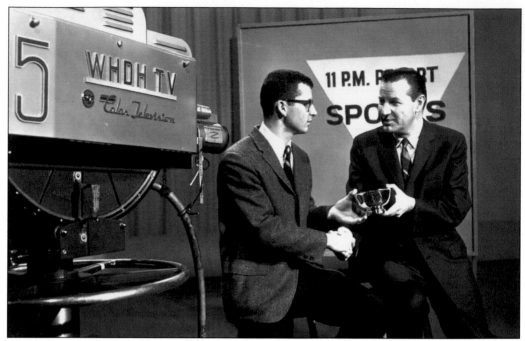

BRUCE FENNIE WITH DON GILLIS OF CHANNEL 5. The growing recognition of the Terrier program was evidenced by a Bruce Fennie television appearance with local sports legend Don Gillis (right). Gillis was a pioneer on the local sports scene as Boston's first sports anchor.

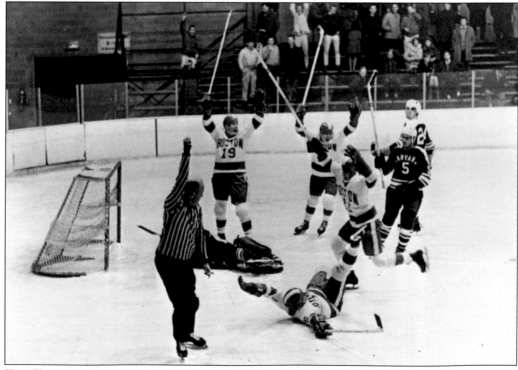

THE TERRIERS SCORE AGAINST HARVARD. With sticks in the air, the Terriers celebrate a goal versus Harvard. On the ice is Dennis O'Connell.

JACK FERREIRA '66. Jack Ferreira was Boston University hockey's equivalent to the Bruins' "Mr. Zero," Frank Brimsek. A catalyst in the Terriers' rise to prominence under coach Jack Kelley, Ferreira took over the net-minding position in his sophomore year as a member of Kelley's first recruiting class. His eight shutouts as a junior in 1964–1965 remain a Terrier single-season record, as does his 15 career shutouts in 78 career games. Upon his graduation, both were also league (ECAC) records. Ferreira's miraculous save on Boston College's Bob Kupka in the 1966 Beanpot Tournament opening round with the Terriers trailing 3-1 is acknowledged as the single biggest momentum swing in Terrier hockey annals. Ferreira was immortalized by New York Times sportswriting icon Red Smith in a memorable 1966 column "Legally Blind, But Top Goalie." Ferreira has enjoyed a long, prosperous career in the National Hockey League as a scout, general manager, and personnel director. The Providence, Rhode Island, native is a member of the Boston University Hall of Fame.

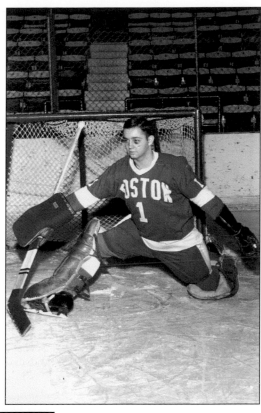

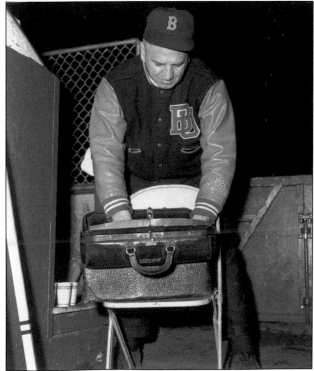

TONY DOUGAL. As the longtime team athletic trainer, Tony Dougal attained legendary status among Boston University skaters. His bag always contained the appropriate remedy for whatever ailed the Terriers.

35

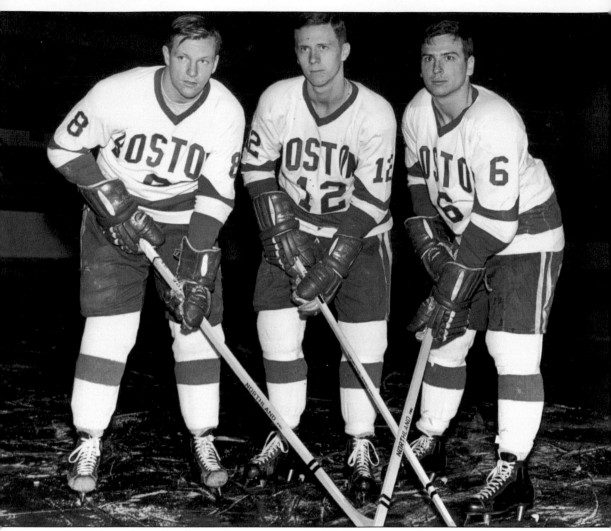

JIM WOOD '67, JIM QUINN, '67, AND MIKE SOBESKI '67. In their junior year, from left to right, Jim Wood, Jim Quinn, and Mike Sobeski put up some impressive numbers during the 1965–1966 season. Quinn's line of 24-25-49 placed him third on the team, while Sobeski's of 18-21-39 placed him fifth overall. Wood, the brother of former major league pitcher Wilbur Wood, had his best offensive season, with 10-17-27.

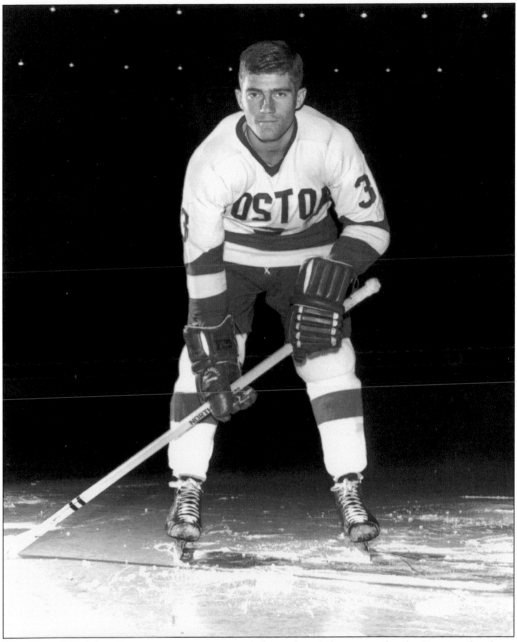

Tom Ross '66. Tom Ross was a no-nonsense defense-first defenseman for the Terriers for three seasons from 1963 to 1966. He was the MVP of the 1966 Terrier Beanpot championship, and a central figure in the Terriers' resurgence and return to the NCAA tournament in 1966. He is a member of the Boston University Hall of Fame.

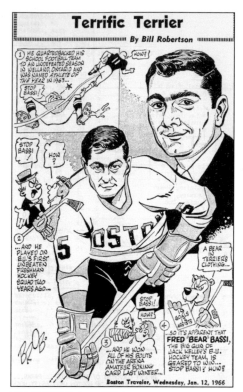

Terrific Terrier

By Bill Robertson

① HE QUARTERBACKED HIS SCHOOL FOOTBALL TEAM TO AN UNDEFEATED SEASON IN WELLAND, ONTARIO AND WAS NAMED ATHLETE OF THE YEAR IN 1963...

HOW? STOP BASSI!

STOP BASSI HOW?

STOP BASSI! HOW?

② ...AND HE PLAYED ON B.U.'S FIRST UNBEATEN FRESHMAN HOCKEY SQUAD TWO YEARS AGO...

A BEAR IN TERRIER'S CLOTHING...

③ ...AND HE WON ALL OF HIS BOUTS ON THE AREA'S AMATEUR BOXING CARD LAST WINTER...

④ 80 GOALS & ASSISTS

...SO IT'S APPARENT THAT **FRED 'BEAR' BASSI**, THE BIG GUN OF JACK KELLEY'S B.U. HOCKEY TEAM, IS GEARED TO WIN... STOP BASSI & HOW?

Boston Traveler, Wednesday, Jan. 12, 1966

FRED BASSI '67. A native of Niagara Falls, Ontario, Fred "Bear" Bassi '67 remains one of the Terriers' most prolific offensive and colorful players of all time. An imposing on-ice presence, Bassi possessed a sniper's scoring touch, as evidenced by 80 career goals (61 assists). Plagued by injuries as a senior, the Bear's junior year was his best. Skating on the Terriers' explosive "gray line" with Bruce Fennie and Dennis O'Connell, he led the team in both goals (35) and total points (64). For his efforts, Bassi was named All-America, team MVP, and New England's Most Outstanding Forward. Shown with him is Boston College Hall of Famer John Cuniff (lower right), the Terriers most honored opponent in 1966. Bassi was a Golden Gloves boxer prior to coming to Boston University and landed a memorable haymaker on Harvard's Tag Demment during an infamous brawl in the 1966 Beanpot Tournament final, which was won by the Terriers 9-2.

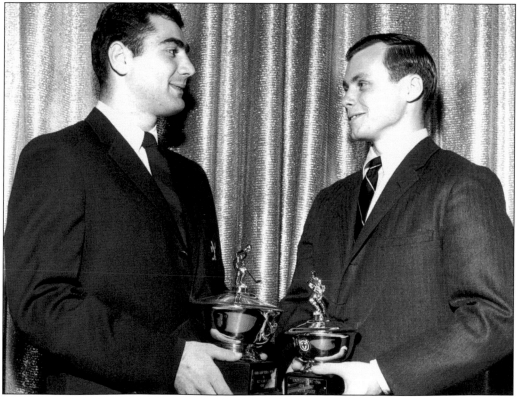

DENNIS O'CONNELL '66. The captain of the 1965–1966 team, Dennis O'Connell, a native of South Boston, led the Terriers both on and off the ice with his exemplary work ethic. O'Connell was a diligent defensive forward and improved his offensive production each year, totaling 29-51-80 in 65 games as a junior and senior. After two straight championship game losses to Boston College and his Southie neighbor John Cunniff (the 1964 and 1965 tournament MVP), O'Connell had the privilege of accepting the 1966 Beanpot trophy as captain on behalf of his teammates. His victory lap holding the trophy aloft to the Boston University corner of the Boston Garden began a tournament tradition. He is a past chairman of the the Friends of Boston University Hockey.

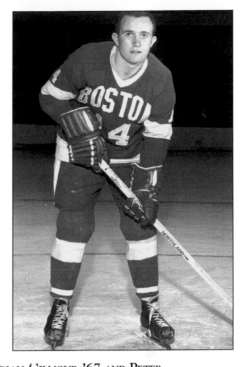

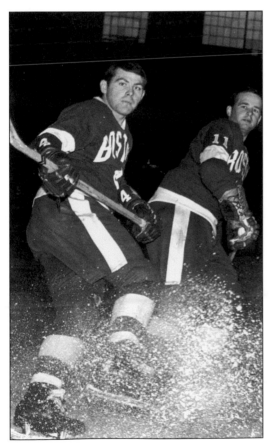

BRIAN GILMOUR '67 AND PETER MCLACHLAN '67. Brian Gilmour (left) personified the term student-athlete. As a smooth-skating, offensively skilled defenseman, his career totals of 36-87-123 made him the Terriers' all-time assist leader. A first team All-American his senior year on the Terriers' Beanpot championship and NCAA semifinalist team, he also excelled off the ice: he was a dean's list student; the 1967 E. Ray Speare Award winner, presented annually to the university's top student-athlete; and the first student-athlete to be named president of the Scarlet Key, the All-University Honorary Activities Society. He spent most of his career paired defensively with his cousin, Peter McLachlan. McLachlan averaged 1 point per game, posting career numbers of 26-70-96. He was a key contributor to Terrier squads that combined for a record of 52-13-1 during his final two varsity seasons. A co-captain of the 1967 team, he closed out his Terrier tenure as a first-team All-East selection. Off the ice, McLachlan was inducted into the School of Management Hall of Fame for academic and student leadership. In 2001, he and Gilmour were inducted into the university Hall of Fame.

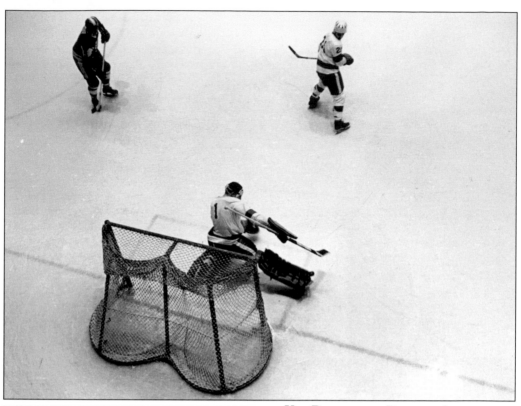

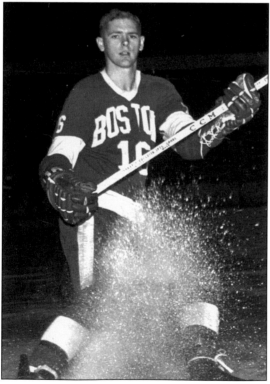

KEN DRYDEN AND DARRELL ABBOTT AT THE 1966 ARENA TOURNAMENT. The 1966 Boston Arena Christmas Tournament never crowned a champion but established a legend. Boston University and Cornell, the Athens and Sparta of eastern college hockey at the time, played a 3-3 double-overtime tie in the tournament championship match. The performance of Cornell sophomore goalie Ken Dryden (above) was immense in his first encounter with Boston University, setting the tone for three years of Terrier frustration. An unlikely offensive hero for the Terriers in the game was sophomore defenseman Darrell Abbott (left), as his wrist shot, clear-in attempt from center ice somehow eluded the Cornell goalie. The two teams met again in the ECAC and NCAA championship games, both won by Dryden and the Big Red.

A WAYNE RYAN CARTOON. Goalie Wayne Ryan '67 played sparingly his first two years as a Terrier, backing up before taking over as the starter in 1966–1967. Ryan wound up putting together an All-American caliber season (20-5-1, with a 2.67 GAA and .900 save percentage), backstopping the Terriers to the Beanpot Tournament championship and ECAC and NCAA title games. Cartoonist Phil Bissell began producing an annual cartoon depicting the Terrier seniors in 1964–1965. The tradition lives on today, and the cartoon is unveiled at the annual Friends of Boston University Hockey banquet.

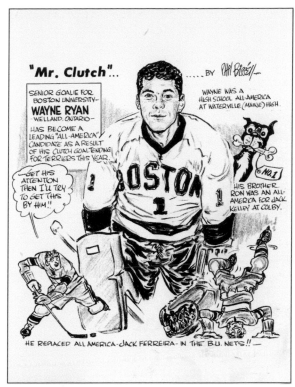

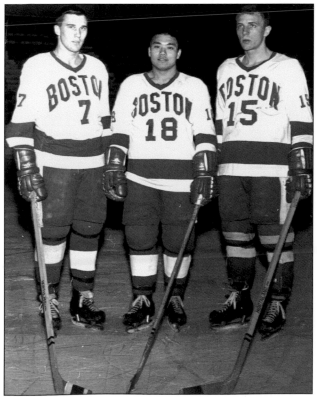

THE "PINBALL LINE." The trio of left wing Serge Boily (7), center Herb Wakabayashi (18), and right wing Mickey Gray (15) remains one of the most prolific offensive lines in Terrier hockey history. Dubbed the "Pinball Line" for their pinpoint passing ability, the unit's 170 point total—Wakabayashi (16-51-67), Boily (29-26-55), and Gray (24-24-48)—in 1966–1967 ranks second all-time.

41

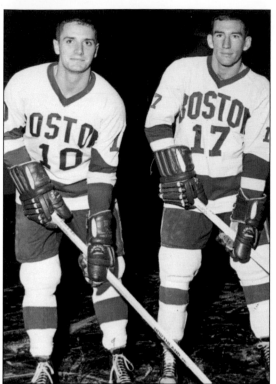

JACK PARKER '68 AND BILLY RILEY '68. Jack Parker (left) spent most of his Terrier career on the same line with classmate Billy Riley. Riley is a member of one of American hockey's most renowned families (Billy's uncle Jack was the legendary Army coach and mentor of the 1960 United States Olympic team's gold medal team), and he went on to a career as the head coach at UMass (Lowell), successfully guiding the program from Division II to Division I and membership in the Hockey East.

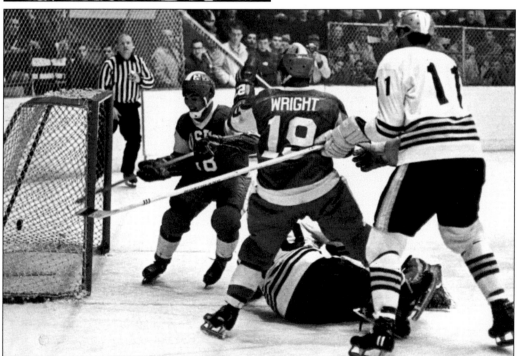

HERB WAKABAYASHI. They may not have been very big, but Herb Wakabayashi (18) and Eddie Wright (19) put relentless pressure on opposing goaltenders. Here, the duo completes a scoring play versus Boston College in action at the Boston Arena during the 1969–1970 season.

BILL HINCH '69. Bill Hinch was a hard-hitting, classic stay-at-home defenseman, and led the 1968–1969 team to a 19-10 record. The Terriers fell short of a coveted NCAA tournament bid as the result of an ECAC semifinal overtime (3-2) loss to Cornell in Ken Dryden's final game versus Boston University.

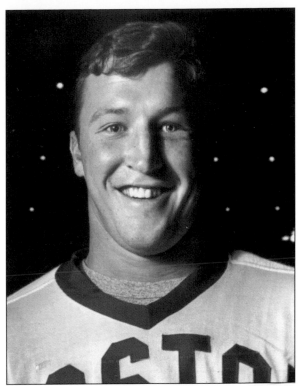

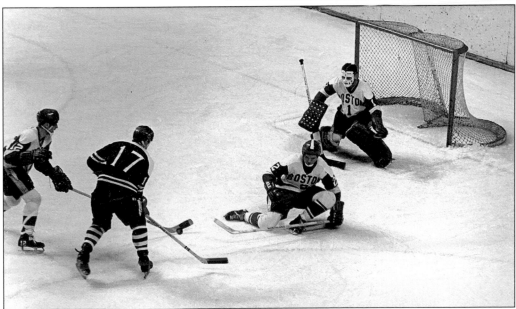

JIM McCANN '69. Jim McCann (right) became the Terriers' number one goalie in 1967–1968, succeeding Wayne Ryan. The former Dedham High School standout won 38 career games and is currently ninth all-time in goals against average, with 2.85. He was the 1968 Beanpot Tournament MVP for the champion Terriers. McCann was a true "iron man" in 1968–1969, playing all but 42 minutes of game action. He went on to become the chairman of the Friends of Boston University Hockey.

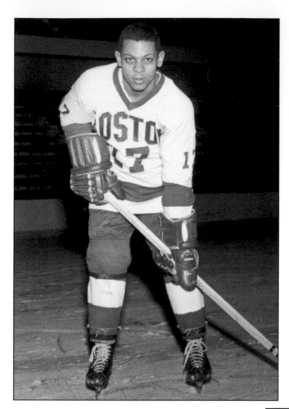

EDDIE WRIGHT '69. Eddie Wright was part of the Terriers' Chatham, Ontario, connection, along with Herb Wakabayashi. Although listed at just 5 feet 4 inches and 135 pounds, Wright played a lot bigger. He was a dervish in the offensive zone combining with Herb Wakabayashi and Serge Boily to form the "UN line" and earned a 29-32-61 record in 61 games his junior and senior years. He went on to become the head coach at the University of Buffalo.

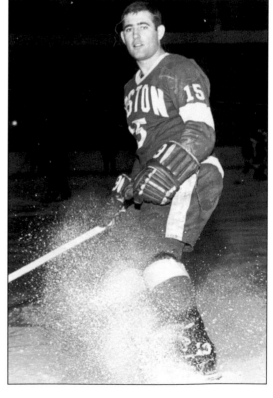

JOHN COOKE '68. John Cooke spent most of his career on a defensive-minded line with classmates Bill Riley and Jack Parker. A native of Regina, Saskatchewan, Cooke is a past chairman of the Friends of Boston University Hockey. His daughter Jillian '02 was the Terrier varsity manager for three seasons.

MIKE HYNDMAN '70. It did not matter what position Mike Hyndman played, he excelled all over the ice. He proved it by leading the nation in scoring one year and being named All-America as a defenseman the next season. Defined by his trademark rocketlike slap shot, Hyndman left Boston University as the all-time leading scorer, with 171 points (52 goals, 119 assists). He scored 67 points in his first varsity campaign, was chosen New England Sophomore of the Year, and led the nation in scoring. After another prolific offensive year up front, Hyndman moved back to the blue line. He was named an All-America in 1970 and was elected to the Terrier Hall of Fame in 1990. Hyndman's booming shot was often compared to a cannon. Below, Hyndman and center Steve Stirling (left) '71 get ready to open fire.

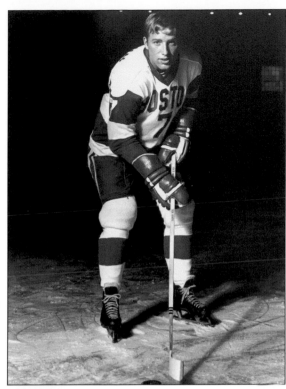

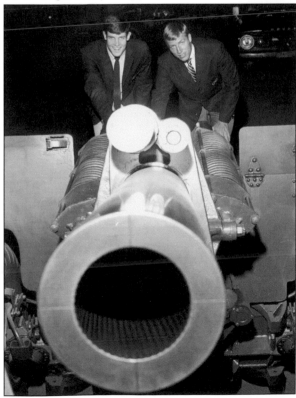

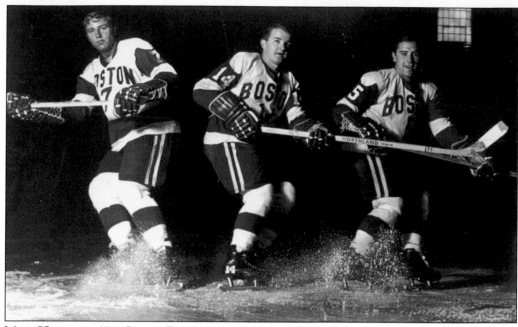

MIKE HYNDMAN '70, LARRY DAVENPORT '70, AND DICK TOOMEY '70. The line of left wing Mike Hyndman, center Larry Davenport, and right wing Dick Toomey ranked one, two, and three in scoring for the 1968–1969 Terriers. Pictured from left to right, the three also rank among the Terriers' all-time scoring leaders—Hyndman (52-119-171), Davenport (67-87-154), and Toomey (51-64-115).

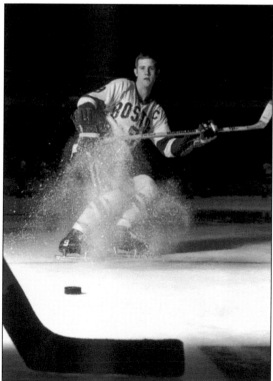

STEVE STIRLING, CAPTAIN OF THE 1970–1971 TEAM. Steve Stirling was one in a long line of smooth, yet tenacious Terrier center icemen. The Ontario native captained and led the Terriers' first National Championship team (1970–1971) in scoring with 27-43-70. Stirling was the 1971 Beanpot Tournament MVP and a member of the NCAA All-Tournament team the same year. He was consistently adept in all three zones. As a head coach, Stirling led the 1985 Providence College Friars to the NCAA title game.

WAYNE GOWING '70. Wayne Gowing was a relatively unheralded member of the Terriers from 1967 to 1970. Gowing was a 10-goal scorer in 1969–1970 as a junior and notched a hat trick in the third period of the 1970 Beanpot Tournament championship game to deliver Boston University a come-from-behind 5-4 victory over Boston College. He has been the longtime head coach at Western Ontario University.

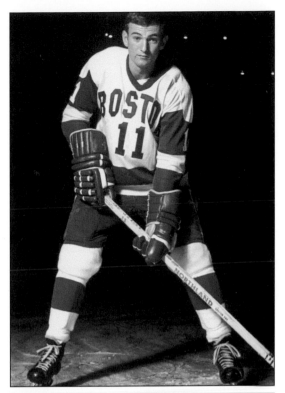

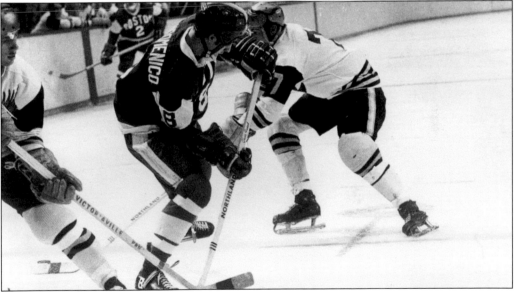

PAUL GIANDEMENICO '72 VERSUS BOSTON COLLEGE IN THE BEANPOT TOURNAMENT. A small, lightning-quick forward and relentless penalty killer, Terrier Paul Giandemenico (of Walpole, Massachusetts) was one of several local members of the program's back-to-back National Championship teams in 1971 and 1972. Seen here in Beanpot Tournament action versus Boston College, Giandemenico received the Frank Jones Award as New England's Best Defensive Forward as a senior. The "Sweeper" played professionally in Italy and became chairman of the Friends of Boston University Hockey.

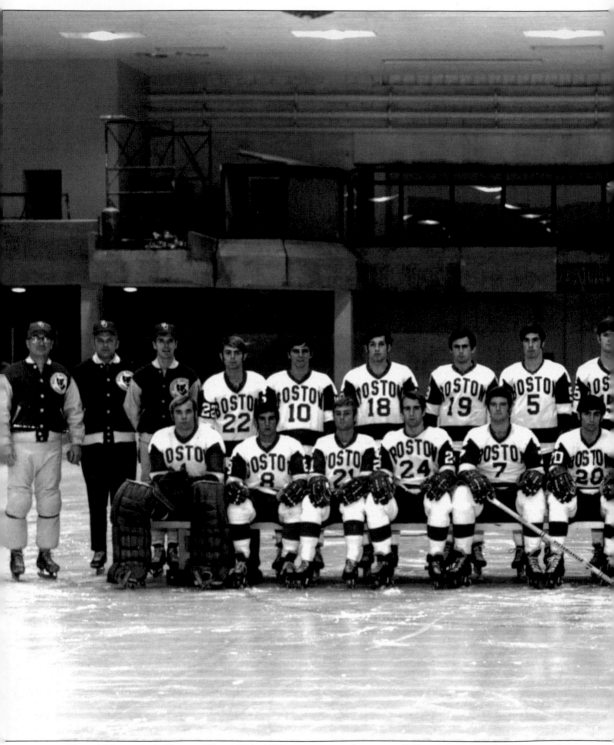

THE 1971–1972 TEAM. The 1971–1972 team won the second Terrier national championship, and remains the last to win back-to-back national titles. Posting a record of 26-4-1, the Terriers allowed a paltry 69 goals. Three members of the team, goalie Dan Brady, defenseman Bob

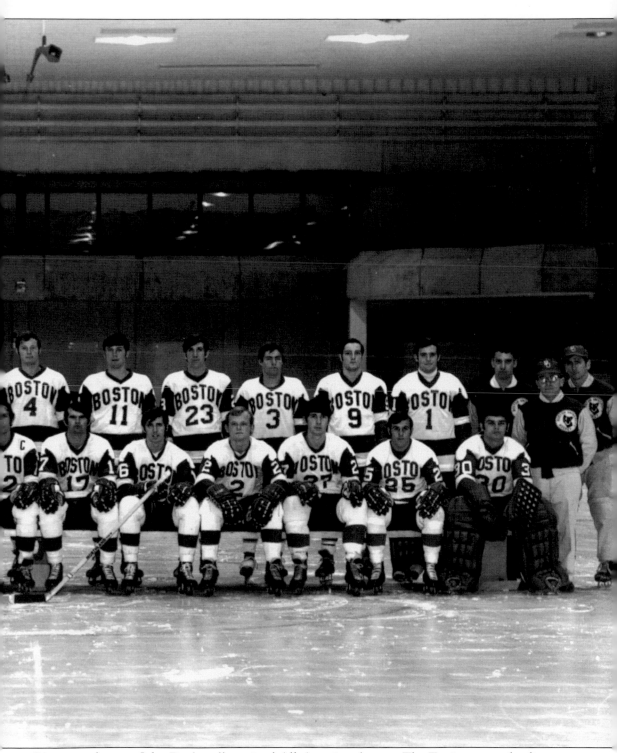

Brown, and center John Danby, all received All-American honors. The Terriers were the first team to capture college hockey's "Triple Crown," winning the Beanpot, ECAC, and NCAA titles in the same season.

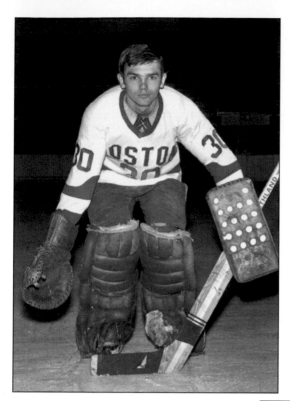

DAN BRADY '72. Dan Brady was half of one of the greatest goaltending duos in college hockey history. As a junior splitting time with classmate Tim Reagan, Brady compiled a 2.04 goals against average as the Terriers won their first National Championship. Brady was named MVP for his tournament performance at Syracuse, New York. For an encore Brady was named first team All-America, All-East, and All-New England as the Terriers won a second consecutive National Championship in 1972. His 2.27 career goals against average remains a Boston University record. He is a Terrier Hall of Famer.

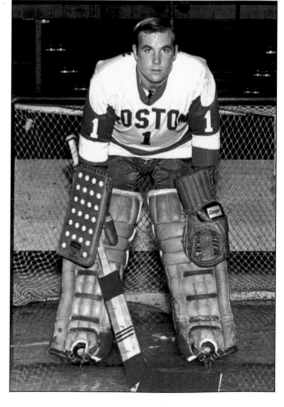

TIM REGAN '72. Tim Regan, a native of Rhode Island, was half of one of college hockey's greatest all-time goaltending tandems. After returning from the 1972 Olympics in Sapporo, Japan, Regan matched the achievement of Brady the previous year by being named the Most Outstanding Player of the 1972 NCAA championships at the Boston Garden, allowing just one goal in two games. Regan ranks second in all-time save percentage (.909) and goals against average (2.39) among Terrier goalies. His season goals against average (1.77) and save percentage (.929) in 1970–1971 remain Boston University records. He is a Terrier Hall of Famer.

JOHN DANBY '72. John "Jake" Danby was a signature player during the Terriers' run of early 1970s dominance. A consummate, all-around center iceman from Port Credit, Ontario, Jake led the teams in goals in each of his three varsity seasons. Danby was the captain of the 1971–1972 "Triple Crown" Terriers (winners of the Beanpot, ECAC, and NCAA championships), and his individual efforts translated into being named MVP of all three tournaments. An All-American, he also received the George V. Brown Award as the Terriers' MVP. Danby is a Boston University Hall of Famer, and his 160 career points rank him third behind only Mike Hyndman and Bob Marquis among three-year varsity players.

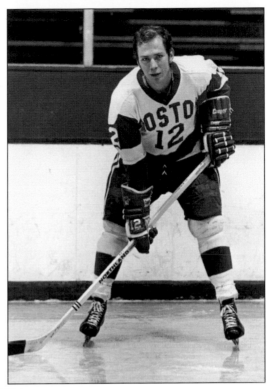

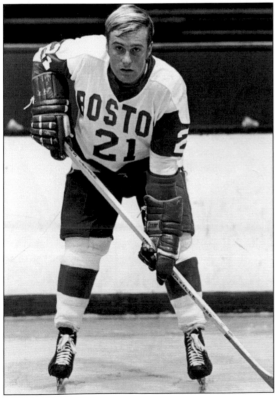

DONALD "TOOT" CAHOON '72. Donald "Toot" Cahoon was a feisty left wing on the top line of the Terriers' consecutive NCAA championship teams (1971, 1972). He often played his best hockey in the Terriers' biggest games. The former Marblehead (Massachusetts) High School multiple-sport star scored a pair of goals versus Denver in the 1971 NCAA semifinal in Syracuse, New York. For his efforts, Cahoon was named to the All-Tournament team. An assistant to Jack Parker on three different occasions, Cahoon coached Princeton to its only ECAC championship and NCAA appearances. He is currently the head coach at UMass (Amherst).

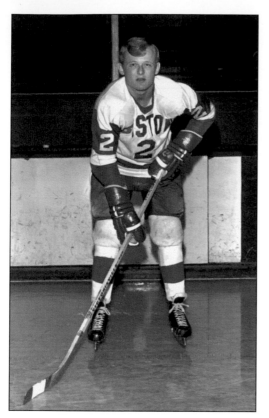

BOB BROWN. Bob Brown, a native of Scarborough, Ontario, was half of one of the greatest defensive tandems in college hockey history. Playing only two varsity seasons, Brown set a scoring record for Boston University defensemen (31-79-110) and was named All-America twice. Brown and his defense partner Ric Jordan simply controlled games whenever they were on the ice, particularly on the power play. A suffocating defender, Brown's booming slap shot and puck-carrying skills were virtually unmatched in the college game—with the notable exception of Jordan. A Terrier Hall of Famer, Brown signed with the fledgling World Hockey Association's New England Whalers after his junior season.

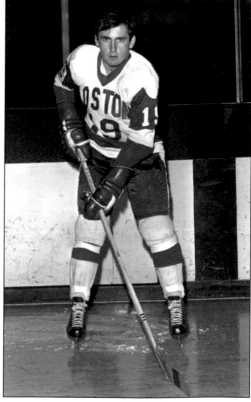

RON ANDERSON. Ron Anderson was a crafty center man from Moncton, New Brunswick, and scored 87 points (39-48-87) for the back-to-back NCAA championship teams in 1971 and 1972. Anderson was elected a co-captain for the 1972–1973 season but instead signed a pro contact and played for his old Boston University coach, Jack Kelley, for the World Hockey Association's New England Whalers. Anderson also played in the NHL for the Washington Capitals. As a head coach, Anderson had the distinction of coaching Merrimack College to the NCAA tournament. He is currently a scout for the Chicago Blackhawks.

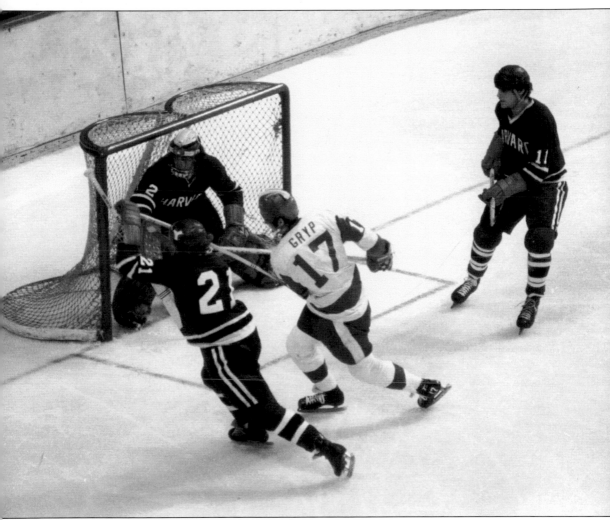

Bob Gryp '72. Bob Gryp (17), shown here in action versus Harvard and goalie Joe Bertagna (the current Hockey East commissioner), was a burly left wing who was among the top scorers on the 1971 and 1972 NCAA championship teams. Gryp was the third leading scorer (9-36-45) and tied for the team lead in assists with Bob Brown on the 1971–1972 team. Gryp spent time in the NHL with both the Boston Bruins and Washington Capitals from 1973 to 1976.

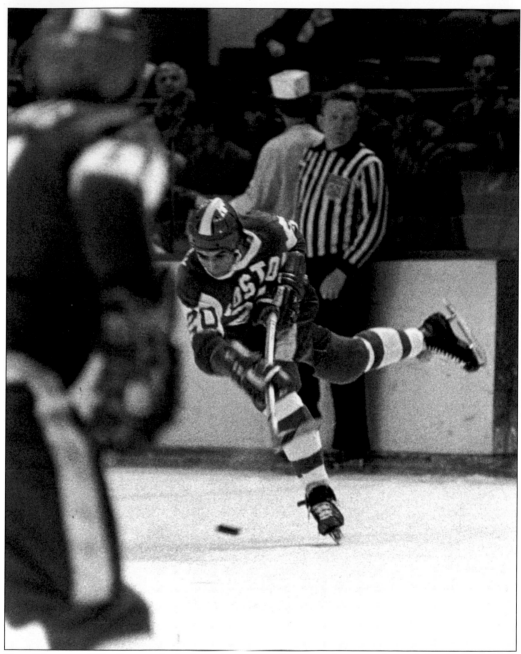

BOB MURRAY '72. From relatively unknown walk-on to key member of the back-to-back National Champions defensive corps, Bob Murray from Quincy, Massachusetts, became quite a success story. Paired with Quebec native Mike LaGarde '72, the solid defense-first tandem was the "other" regular defensive pairing for the Terrier teams that featured All-Americans Bob Brown and Ric Jordan. The unassuming stay-at-home style of Murray and LaGarde was a sharp contrast to the flamboyance of Brown and Jordan. Both were highly efficient in their own way. A longtime assistant coach to Jack Parker, attorney Bob Murray has worked as a sports agent for two decades representing numerous former Terrier skaters.

Four
THE PARKER ERA BEGINS (1973–1989)

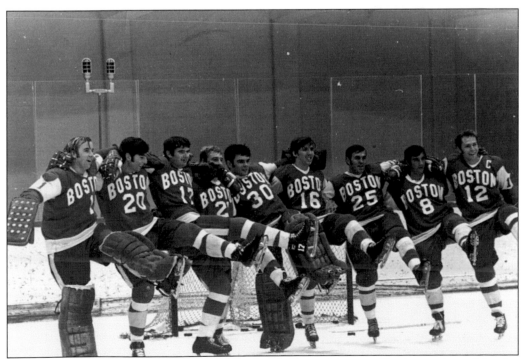

THE 1971–1972 TERRIER CHORUS LINE. Is this *A Chorus Line* or a Terrier version of the Ice Follies? Actually, it is the nine members of the 1972 Terrier senior class. Pictured, from left to right, are Tim Regan, Bob Murray, Bob Gryp, Donald "Toot" Cahoon, Dan Brady, Guy Burrowes, Pete "Thunder" Thornton, Paul "Sweeper" Giandemenico, and John "Jake" Danby. They had a combined record of 54-6-2 through their final two seasons at Boston University.

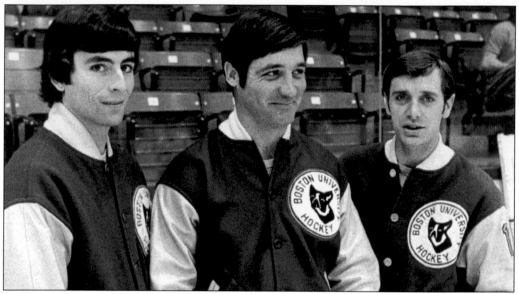

THE 1972–1973 COACHING STAFF. There were changes on Babcock Street for the 1972–1973 season. Coach Jack Kelley had departed for the World Hockey Association (WHA) after a brilliant decade as head coach. The new man in charge was Leon Abbott (center), the former head coach at Rensselaer Polytechnic Institute. The selection came as somewhat of a surprise. Abbott remained only a season and a half. An eligibility controversy involving NCAA violations clouded his brief tenure as Terrier head coach. Abbott is flanked by his young assistants Bob Murray (left) and Jack Parker.

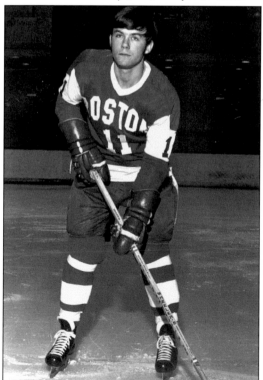

DAVE WISENER, CAPTAIN 1972–1973. Dave Wisener skated a regular shift for the 1971–1972 NCAA championship teams. In the aftermath of the departure of co-captains elect Ron Anderson and Ric Jordan to the WHA, Wisener became the Terrier captain his senior year. The steady left wing from Pictou, Nova Scotia, had a solid offensive season with 21-20-41 totals. More importantly, he held the team together through the difficult eligibility controversy that forced the Terriers to forfeit 11 games.

STEVE DOLOFF '73. Steve Doloff moved up the Terrier line chart at the center position through his Terrier career. As a sophomore and junior, the clever center man from Melrose, Massachusetts, contributed 24-41-65 to the Boston University offense. As a senior, Doloff's 16-36-52 scoring line earned him All-American honors, following in the strides of Steve Stirling and John Danby, his former teammates of the same position.

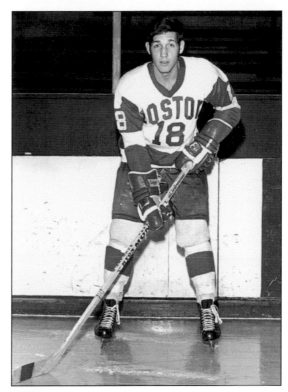

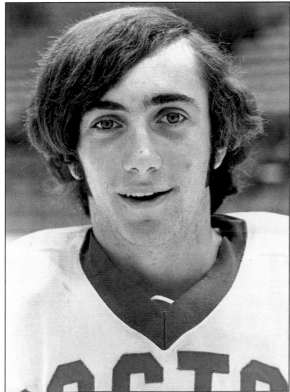

PAUL O'NEIL. Paul O'Neil spent just one season in scarlet and white, but what a season it was! After a season with the Terrier junior varsity team, O'Neil exploded on the scene with 35 goals and 53 points. His goal total moved him to the number three position for a single season behind All-Americans Jack Garrity (51) and Bob Marquis (41). His total still ties him for fifth best some 30 years later.

57

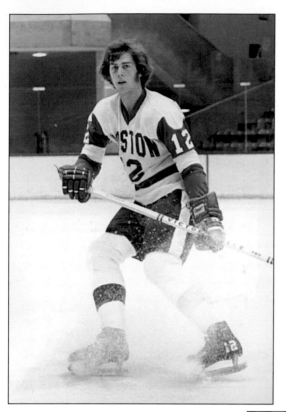

DICK DeCLOE. Dick DeCloe played only 14 games in his Terrier career. A challenge to his eligibility based on the acceptance of room-and-board money as a junior hockey player in Ontario resulted in DeCloe being declared ineligible. The Terriers were forced to forfeit the 11 games they won with DeCloe in the lineup. Subsequent court rulings related to other eligibility cases with similar circumstances vindicated DeCloe.

BILL BUCKTON '76. Bill Buckton and his teammate Peter Marzo '76 are forever linked in Terrier hockey history. The Buckton-Marzo case was the second eligibility case involving Canadian junior hockey to affect the Boston University program, and it resulted in a much different decision. An injunction was granted that allowed the two players to finish their careers at Boston University without any further challenge to their eligibility. Marzo became a prolific offensive center, leading the team in scoring in 1973–1974 with 46 points. He went on to career totals of 58-80-138 in 94 games. A feisty winger, Buckton finished his career just shy of the Boston University "Century Club" with 45-47-92 totals. The Buckton-Marzo decision proved to be a significant one in the subsequent perception of junior hockey with regard to college hockey.

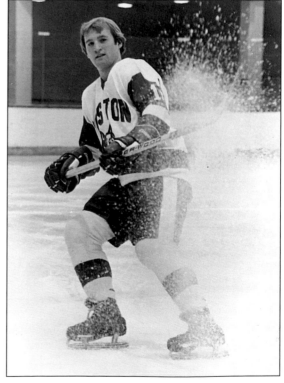

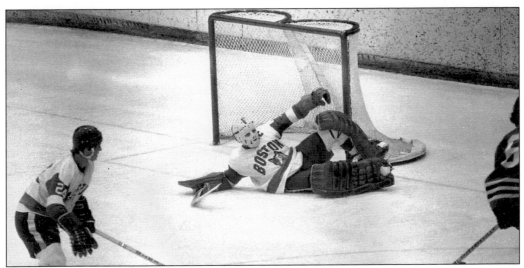

ED WALSH '74. As was the case at Boston University during the 1970s, future All-Americans waited their turn. Ed Walsh was no exception. As a sophomore in 1972, Walsh was the number three goalie behind All-Americans and future Boston University Hall of Famers Tim Regan and Dan Brady. The following year, Walsh burst from the shadows and posted a 20-6-1 record with a 2.91 goals against average and .911 save percentage. His performance allowed him to follow Brady's All-American recognition with his own selection. Quick and highly competitive, Walsh lowered his goals against average to 2.87 and matched his save percentage number, leading the Terriers back to the NCAA tournament and to their first of four ECAC titles. Walsh was the first winner of the Eberly Award in 1974 as the Beanpot Tournament's top goalie. Here, Walsh defends his territory in the Beanpot versus Harvard, as defenseman Bob Sunderland (24) moves in to help out.

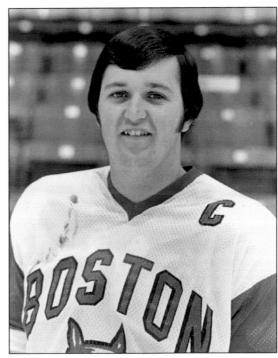

VIC STANFIELD '75. Blessed with tremendous hands, Vic Stanfield, the captain of the 1975–1976 team, still holds strong in the Terrier record book. His 60 assists as a senior remain the Boston University standard. His 129 career helpers place him first among defensemen and third all-time. He also ranks first in points (160) on the list of Terrier defensemen. Stanfield was a deft passer and brilliant power play performer. He led the 1975 repeat ECAC champions in scoring, with 10-60-70, outdistancing all his teammates on the forward lines. His single-season point total ranks fifth all-time. He was the first defenseman and second player ever to be named Beanpot Tournament MVP twice (1973 and 1975). A golf professional, Stanfield recently designed a course in New Hampshire. He is a member of both the Boston University and Beanpot Halls of Fame.

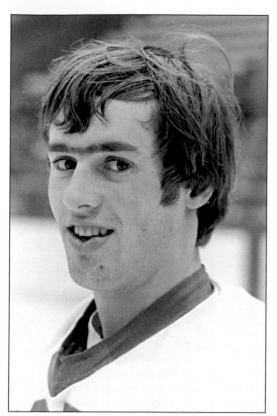

CAPTAIN BILL BURLINGTON '75. Bill Burlington, the captain of the 1974–1975 Terriers, sustained the line of four consecutive All-American centers, being so honored as a junior in 1974. A small but shifty center, Burlington excelled as a playmaker, amassing 76 assists in three varsity seasons. The 1974–1975 Boston University team won a second consecutive ECAC championship and advanced to the NCAA championships in St. Louis.

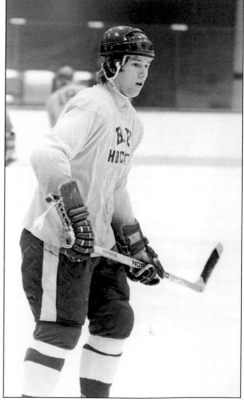

MIKE FIDLER. Mike Fidler was a local high school star for Malden Catholic's state championship team, and took his power forward game to Babcock Street for two impact seasons. As a key member of the 1975 and 1976 back-to-back ECAC champions, Fidler racked up a record of 46-48-94 in just 60 games. Mike turned professional after his sophomore year. He played in the NHL for four teams before his career was cut short by a chronic shoulder injury.

PETER BROWN '76. Peter Brown's final three seasons in scarlet and white produced three ECAC championships, three NCAA tournament appearances, and an overall record of 74-18-1. Brown was the Gordon "Mickey" Cochrane Award winner as Boston University's athlete of the year in 1976 and was also a three-time All-East selection and All-America selection his junior year. He remains second to only Vic Stanfield '75 in career assists among Boston University defensemen, with 122. Brown was a Greater Boston state champion at Norwood High School and was later named to the ECAC All-Decade second team.

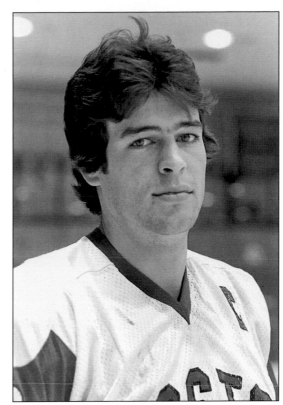

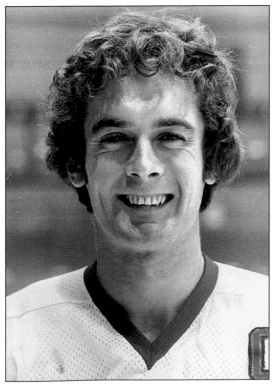

TERRY MEAGHER '76. The oldest of the three Meagher brothers, Terry co-captained the 1975–1976 team with Peter Brown. Playing on three straight ECAC championship teams, Meagher capped his career by leading the team in scoring in 1976 (30-25-55). He was a classy player and leader, and one of the least penalized players in Boston University hockey history, with a mere 40 minutes in his 92-game career. His career offensive totals (74-68-142) still place him in Boston University's top 25 all-time. As the head coach at Bowdoin College, Meagher has consistently placed the Polar Bears among the top Division III programs in the nation.

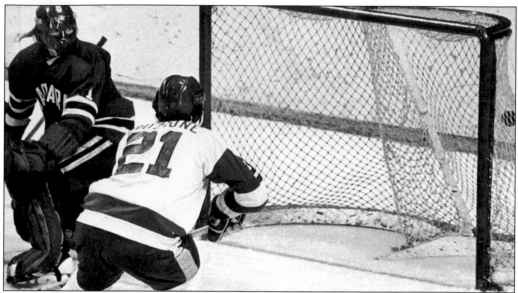

MIKE ERUZIONE '77. Mike Eruzione established himself as a winner during his Boston University career. Often combining with close friend Rick Meagher the left wing from nearby Winthrop, Massachusetts played on four consecutive ECAC Championship teams that made four straight NCAA appearances under head coach Jack Parker. A dogged, relentless player, Eruzione finished his career with 208 points on 92 goals and 116 assists. The total was good for second all-time, two points behind Meagher.

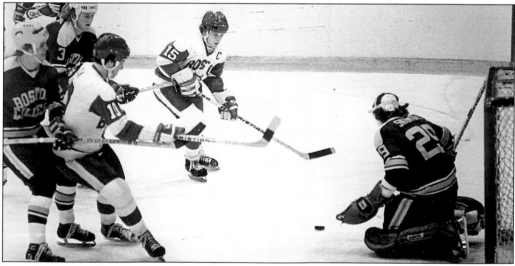

RICK MEAGHER '77. Rick Meagher is Boston University's only three-time All-American. The native of Belleville, Ontario, closed out his career with an 80-point season in 1976–1977. Meagher was a member of four consecutive ECAC championship teams at his center position, often flanked on the left wing by co-captain Mike Eruzione. As a senior, Meagher racked up 6 game-winning, 11 power-play, and 15 go-ahead goals. He finished his career as Boston University's all-time leading scorer, with a record of 90-120-210—2 points ahead of Eruzione. He was a tenacious center in the NHL, often assigned to players like Wayne Gretzky, and was honored with the Frank Selke Award as the league's best defensive forward. Meagher was a first-team ECAC all-decade selection and is a member of the university Hall of Fame.

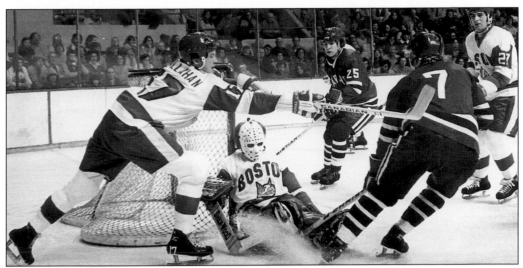

JACK O'CALLAHAN AND BRIAN DUROCHER, CO-CAPTAINS 1977–1978. The co-captains of the 1978 National Championship team, defenseman Jack O'Callahan '79 and goalie Brian Durocher '78, weather a Crimson storm in Beanpot Tournament action at the Boston Garden. Durocher became the Terrier starter as a freshman, succeeding All-American Ed Walsh. His career record of 47-13-1 (.779) places him sixth on the Terriers' all-time goaltending list. Durocher, a great nephew of former major league baseball manager Leo Durocher, enjoyed a successful college coaching career at Colgate and Brown. He is currently the associate head coach of the Terriers. Two-time captain O'Callahan is one of the only junior captains in Terrier history. The Charlestown, Massachusetts, native was a fixture on the blue line throughout his four-year career and was named the 1978 Beanpot Tournament MVP, his best overall offensive season, with a record of 8-47-55. His assist total (47) led the club. He was selected as an All-American in 1979. He went on to win a gold medal with the 1980 United States Olympic "Miracle on Ice" squad before commencing an eight-year NHL career in Chicago and New Jersey.

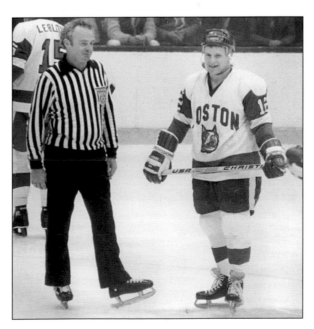

MARK FIDLER '81. Mark Fidler (right), shown sharing an inside joke with then ECAC referee and later Hockey East chief of officials Dana Hennigar, exploded on the college hockey scene with a 30-35-65 season as a freshman to lead the 1977–1978 National Champions in scoring. For the next three years, the offensively gifted former Matignon High School star continued to lead the Terriers in scoring each year. Fidler's point total of 178 (77 goals and 101 assists) still places him eighth all-time at Boston University some 20 years later.

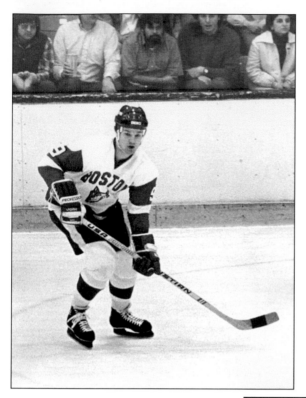

JOHN BETHEL. John Bethel closely followed Mark Fidler in second place on the Terriers' 1977–1978 scoring list, with 63 points (25 goals and 38 assists). After a junior year curtailed by injuries, Bethel turned professional. He later played in the NHL for the Winnipeg Jets.

DAVE SILK. Dave Silk personified the term impact freshman. He was a member of the 1976–1977 ECAC championship team, a championship won for the fourth time in a row. The quick-trigger right wing played most of the season on a line with three-time All-American Rick Meagher, and buried 35 goals to lead the team, a figure that still ties him for fifth on the all-time single season list. The former Thayer Academy sniper followed up with a 27-31-58 record his second year as a Terrier. His blast off a drop pass from Meagher for the game-winning goal in the 1977 ECAC semifinal game versus number one–seeded Clarkson University completed an amazing Boston University rally. The Terriers came back from a two-goal deficit in the final 2 minutes and 30 seconds to win the game 7-6. Silk went on to a gold medal in Lake Placid, New York, before spending eight seasons in the NHL.

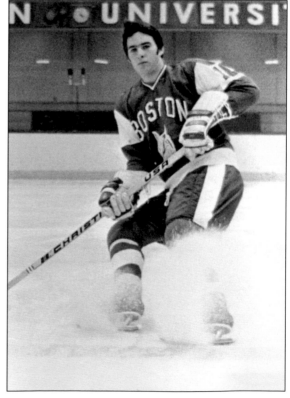

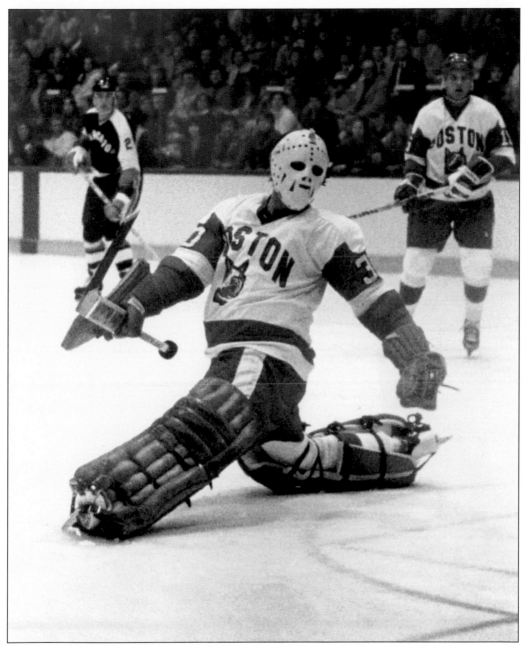

JIM CRAIG '79. The ability, poise, and confidence that goalie Jim Craig displayed in Lake Placid, New York, came as no surprise to those hockey aficionados who had seen Craig perform previously at Boston University. Stepping in as the regular net-minder his rookie year, he helped take the team to a fourth straight ECAC championship and NCAA tournament appearance. In his second year, he split the net-minding chores with senior Brian Durocher and racked up a perfect 16-0-0 record as the Terriers won their third national championship of the decade. In his final season at Boston University, Craig was named All-America. His career record of 50-10-3 is one that may never be equaled. He is a Boston University Hall of Famer. The Terrier defender is Bill LeBlond '80 (right).

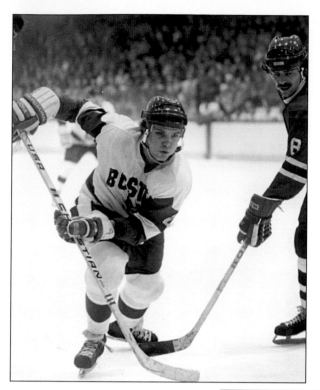

MARC HETNIK '79. Marc Hetnik was a prototypical Terrier center man. The local product from Brookline, Massachusetts, was a relentless fore-checker and dogged penalty killer. He narrowly missed membership in the 100-point club, with a 33-59-92 scoring line.

DICK LAMBY. Dick Lamby transferred from Salem State College after playing for the 1976 Olympic team in Innsbruck, Austria. The powerful skating defenseman played for just one and a half seasons, and took up residence immediately on the Terrier power play. With a propensity for carrying the puck from his blue line position, Lamby racked up 104 points (24 goals and 80 assists) in just 54 career games. Lamby went on to play in the NHL for the St. Louis Blues.

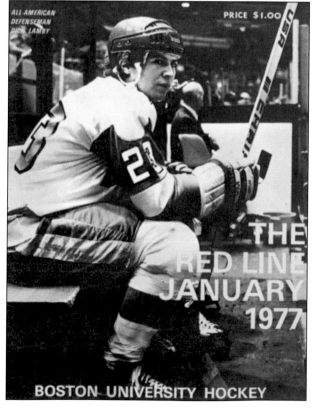

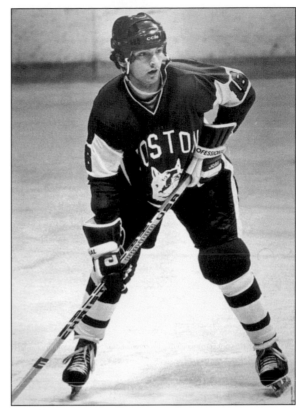

MICKEY MULLEN '79 AND DARYL MACLEOD '81. Through their 26 Beanpot tournament championships, the Terriers have featured a multitude of heroes. It has not only been the All-Americans that have grabbed center-stage recognition. In the 1978 final, Mickey Mullen (right) scored three of his nine goals for the season versus Harvard in the tournament final to lead the Boston University offensive attack. Daryl MacLeod (below) fit the same mold in 1979, scoring two of his eight goals for the season in Beanpot play and adding two assists to lead the Terriers in tournament scoring. The Melrose, Massachusetts, native was named MVP for his efforts.

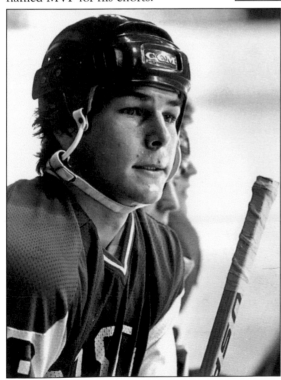

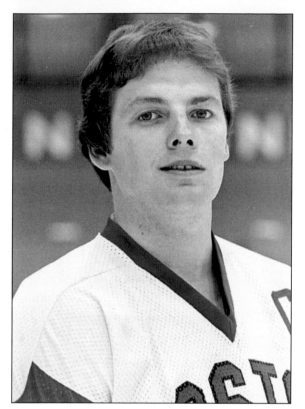

TONY MEAGHER '80. The third in the line of, arguably, the first family of Terrier hockey to be named captain, Tony Meagher carved his own niche at Boston University. As a freshman, the affable Meagher rescued the 0-for-5 Terriers with a memorable overtime game-winning goal in a 6-5 win at Harvard's Watson Rink. The victory turned the Terriers around and pointed them to a fourth straight ECAC crown.

BILL WHELTON. Defenseman Bill "Wally" Whelton followed Jack O'Callahan from nearby Charlestown to Walter Brown Arena. Whelton, a rangy blue liner with a consistent all-around game, led all the Terrier defensemen in scoring in 1979–1980. Turning professional following his junior year, Whelton played for the NHL's Winnipeg Jets and in several European countries.

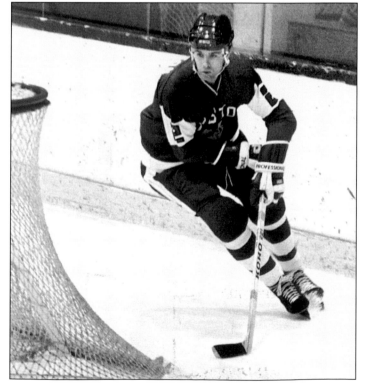

PAUL FENTON '82. Paul Fenton remains one of the Terriers' best success stories. Fenton was a junior varsity player as a freshman, and his hard work and diligence made him the team's number two scorer as a sophomore. After playing only seven games as a junior due to an injury, the Springfield, Massachusetts, native's desire and determination took over again. Fenton was the senior captain of the 1981–1982 Terriers and reached the 20-goal plateau as Boston University captured the Beanpot trophy for the first time in three years. After graduation, his persistence during his time in the minors led to a decade-long NHL career. He is still in the game as director of player personnel for the NHL's Nashville Predators.

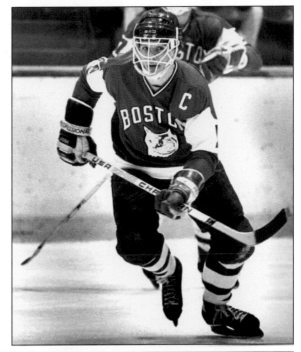

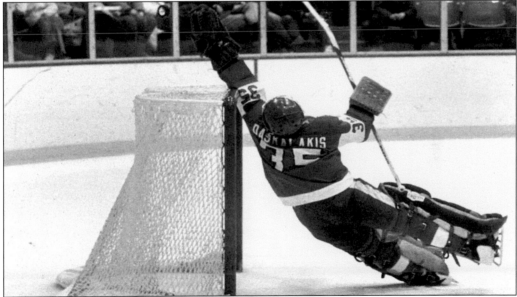

CLEON DASKALAKIS '84. Acrobatic, dynamic, and often spectacular, Cleon Daskalakis resides in elite company among Boston University's all-time greatest goaltenders. He played sparingly his freshman year and established himself as the club's number one net-minder during the 1981–1982 season, leading the Terriers to the Beanpot Tournament championship with a tremendous performance versus Boston College in a 3-1 victory. As a junior, he continued at the forefront of the Terriers' resurgence, as they qualified for the ECAC playoffs for the first time since 1979. He saved his best for last, with a sensational All-American senior performance: a 25-10 record, a 2.92 goals against average, and a .911 save percentage. He went on to play in the NHL for the Boston Bruins.

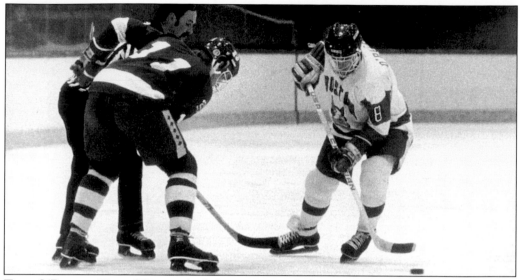

TOM O'REGAN. Tom O'Regan (right) co-captained the 1982–1983 team with his former Matignon High School teammate Jerry August '83. The skillful center iceman led the 1981–1982 team in scoring with a record of 18-34-52 and was named the Beanpot Tournament MVP for his two-goal effort in the Terriers' 3-1 championship game victory over Boston College. After a three-year absence from the ECAC playoffs, O'Regan was instrumental in the Terriers' stretch run to the 1983 postseason, again leading the team in scoring. He was an NHL player for the Pittsburgh Penguins and enjoyed an outstanding decade-long career in the German Elite League.

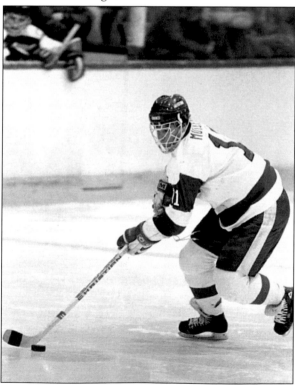

KEVIN MUTCH. Kevin Mutch came to the Terriers in 1981 and promptly averaged one point per game (7-20-27) for the Beanpot champions. A versatile player, "Mutchie" was equally adept at both forward and defense. The Canton, Massachusetts, native was a former Independent School League (ISL) All-Star at St. Sebastian's Prep School and enjoyed his best year on the Terriers' NCAA tournament club in 1983–1984, with a record of 17-12-29. One of the most outgoing and popular players, he went on to coach at his prep school alma mater, St. Sebastian's. He was tragically killed in a Cape Cod pedestrian fatality on Labor Day weekend 1992. The award for the most outstanding player on the winning side in the annual Boston College-Boston University series is named in his memory. He was truly an unforgettable and beloved member of the Terrier hockey family.

MARK PIEROG '84. Mark Pierog (left) was another Terrier who had his best year for the Terriers' ECAC finalist and NCAA tournament team in 1983–1984. Pierog, a native of Ontario, was an important player in all three zones. His 17-17-34 record as a senior placed him second behind John Cullen among Terrier scorers.

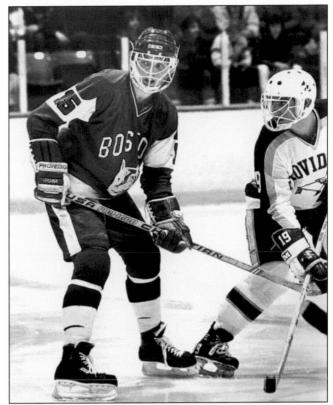

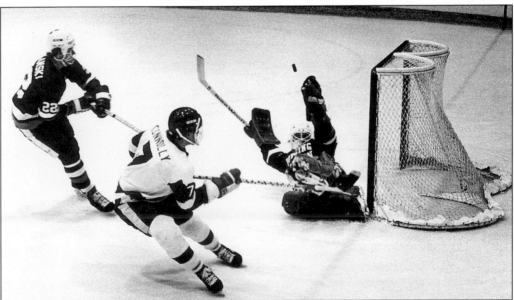

T.J. CONNOLLY '84. T.J. Connolly is pictured here in action versus Bowling Green in the 1984 NCAA tournament at Walter Brown Arena. He was a tough, defensive-minded player for four years. Connolly was a native of Quincy, Massachusetts, and a former Don Bosco star. He captained the 1983–1984 squad that returned to the NCAA tournament for the first time since 1978.

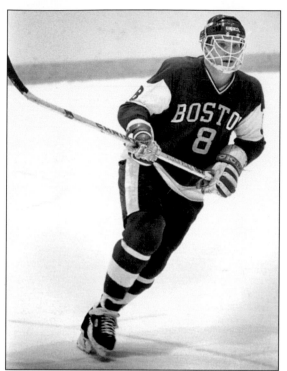

JOE CAPPELLANO. Joe "Cappy" Cappellano was a physical presence on the forward line and always played the game at one speed: breakneck. As a freshman in 1982, his overtime goal at Providence College ended a losing streak in the series. Another in the line of Thayer Academy skaters to come to Boston University, Cappy had his best offensive season in 1983–1984, with a record of 10-24-34.

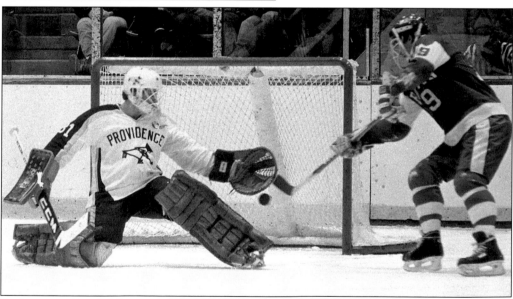

ED LOWNEY '87. Ed Lowney was an often unsung member of the Terriers who very quietly amassed 154 career points (79 goals and 75 assists), ranking him 17th in Terrier hockey annals. His goal total of 79 places him tied for ninth all-time. The Revere, Massachusetts, native was a steady, sound defensive forward with a great touch around the net, often found right in the middle of the big plays in the biggest games. This is evidenced by his tying goal in the 1987 Beanpot Tournament final versus Northeastern University, eventually won in overtime by the Terriers. Here, Lowney (right) scores against future NHL net-minder Chris Terrierri of Providence College.

JOHN CULLEN '87. Fifteen years after his departure from Babcock Street, John Cullen remains the Terriers' all-time leading scorer, with 241 points (98 goals and 143 assists). "Cully" led the team in scoring in all four years and was also a three-time MVP. The crafty center man's junior year was his best offensively (25-49-74), as the Terriers' defeated archrival Boston College for both the Beanpot and Hockey East titles, advancing to the NCAA tournament. As a senior captain, Cullen followed up his All-American campaign by being named a finalist for the Hobey Baker Award, given annually to college hockey's most outstanding player. Cullen went on to an outstanding decade-long (1988–1998) NHL career highlighted by a 110-point season with the Pittsburgh Penguins in 1990–1991. His courageous battle back from cancer in 1998 was recognized by the NHL's prestigious Masterston Award.

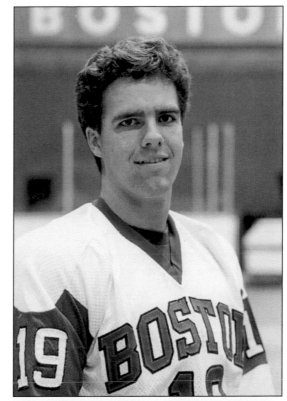

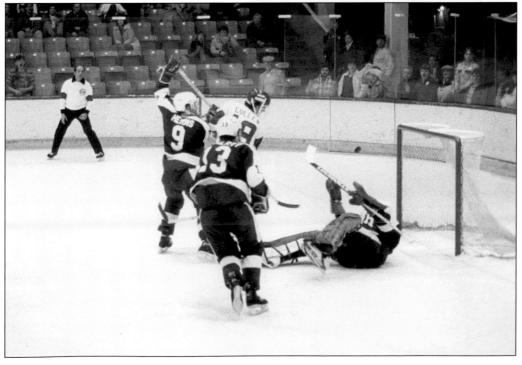

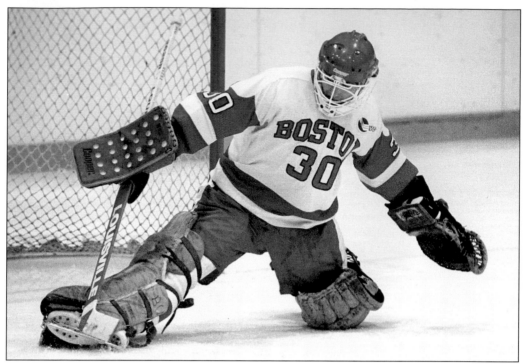

TERRY TAILLEFFER '87 AND BOB DERANEY '87. For three seasons, Terry Tailleffer (above) and Bob Deraney (lower right) split the majority of the playing time in the Terrier net. Though from diverse backgrounds (Tailleffer is from Edmonton, Canada, and Bob Deraney from West Roxbury, Massachusetts), the two complemented each other nicely. Deraney, who became the women's hockey coach at Providence College, posted a 21-12-4 record with a 3.63 goal against average and .888 save percentage for his career. Tailleffer, the 1987 Beanpot MVP and Eberly Award winner, countered with a 38-23-7 record, 3.41 goal against average, and .893 save percentage. His 2,030 career save total places him fourth all-time.

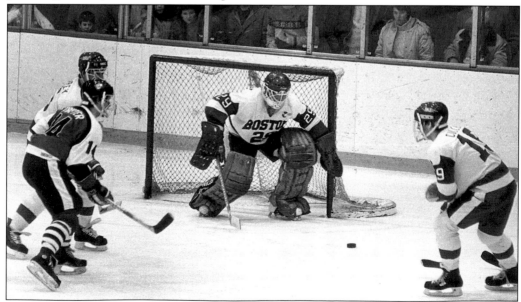

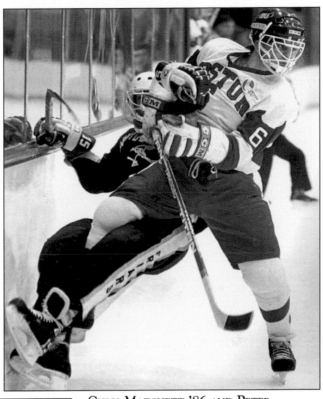

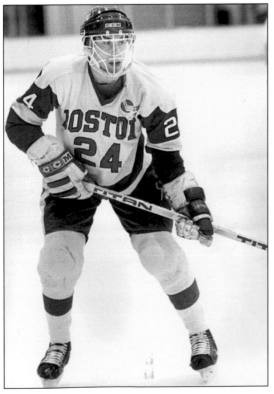

CHRIS MATCHETT '86 AND PETER MARSHALL '86. Defenseman Chris Matchett (above) and center Peter Marshall (left) were two of the very best leaders to ever co-captain the Terriers. Playing at both forward and defense during his career, the smooth-skating Matchett remains one of the most intelligent players to ever skate for the Terriers. Marshall was like a buzz saw at center and excelled as a fore-checker and penalty killer. His best offensive performance was in the 1986 Hockey East title game win over Boston College. Marshall notched a hat trick and skated away with tournament MVP honors as Boston University thumped the Eagles 9-4. He is the only player in Terrier history to be presented with the Bennett McInnis Memorial Award for spirit four years in a row.

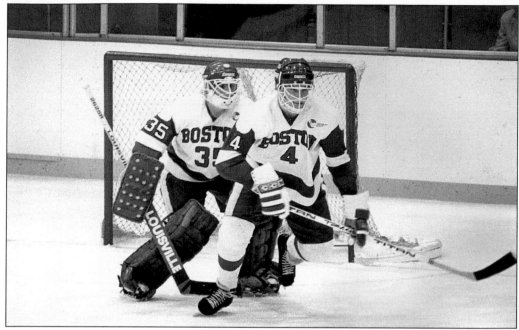

SCOTT SHAUGHNESSY '87. Scott Shaughnessy (right) was an imposing defensive presence as a four-year regular on the blue line. Shown here protecting the net in front of goalie Peter Fish (35), the rugged former St. John's Prep standout often rocked opponents with his physical style. He leveled Boston College forward Bob Sweeney in the opening minute of the 1986 Beanpot final and set the tone for a 4-1 Boston University victory.

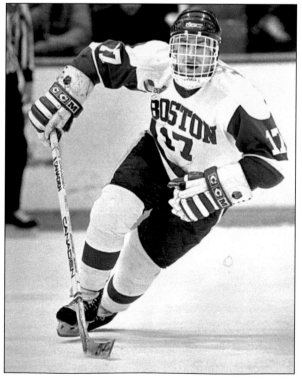

CLARK DONATELLI. Clark Donatelli was a relentless offensive force for the three seasons he spent as a Terrier. Often skating as left wing with John Cullen at center, Donatelli had his best offensive year in 1985–1986. The forward line of Donatelli (28-34-62), Cullen, and Lowney ranks first in total points for a single season with 174. He finished his Terrier career with 65-70-135 offensive totals. A two-time Olympian (1988 and 1992) and team captain (1992), Donatelli played in the NHL for the Minnesota North Stars and Boston Bruins.

SCOTT YOUNG. Scott Young was a number one draft choice of the NHL's Hartford Whalers, which shows why he was regarded so highly during his two years as a Terrier. As proficient in all aspects of the game as anyone to have ever played at Boston University, Young scored 65 points (31 goals and 34 assists) in 71 games. He and Keith Tkachuk are the only Terrier three-time Olympians (1988, 1992, and 2002) in Boston University hockey annals. Young is still skating strong for the NHL's St. Louis Blues, having just completed his 15th season.

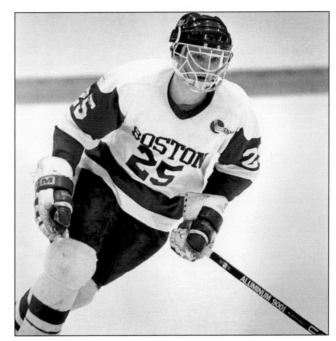

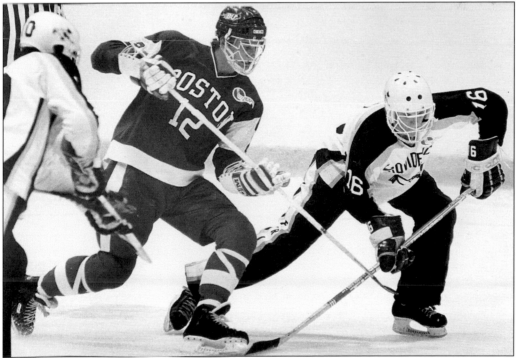

BRAD MACGREGOR. Brad MacGregor '87 was a solid defensive forward and filled the checking role for the Terriers during his career. The native of Edmonton, Canada, is the son of former longtime NHL forward Bruce MacGregor. He saved some of his goals for the biggest games: a game winner versus the University of New Hampshire in the 1984 ECAC playoffs and a two-goal effort in the 1986 Hockey East championship team. MacGregor is currently the director of marketing for the Edmonton Oilers.

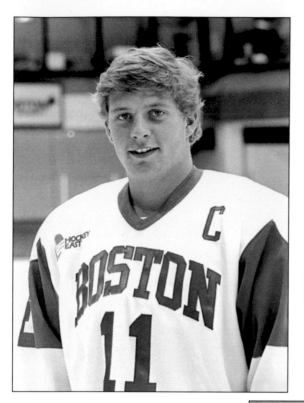

TOM RYAN '88. The 1988 Friends of Hockey banquet was a milestone evening to celebrate the organization's 25th year. On that evening, Tom Ryan, the captain of the 1987–1988 team, swept three major awards including the team MVP and spirit awards. During his Terrier career, Ryan played both defense and forward and provided outstanding leadership as a senior, playing through injuries to take a young team to a third place finish in Hockey East despite professional signing, injuries, and Olympic departures. Ryan was a former star at Newton North High School and is still very much a part of the Terrier hockey scene. He has been the color analyst on the team's radio network with the "Voice of the Terriers" Bernie Corbett.

DAVID QUINN '88. Defenseman David Quinn saw his Terrier career end a year too soon. He was diagnosed with a rare blood disease after his junior year, which ended his playing days at Boston University. A solid three-year regular prior to the diagnosis, Quinn had his best all-around season (2-20-22) as a sophomore in 1985–1986. A number one draft pick of the NHL's Minnesota North Stars, Quinn courageously battled back to play professionally with the benefit of new medication in the early 1990s. A college coach for the past decade, he was recently named the head coach of the USA Development's 17-year-old team.

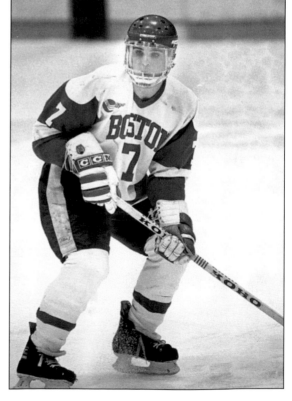

MIKE KELFER '89. Mike Kelfer, the captain of the 1988–1989 team, forever etched his name among the Terriers' all-time pantheon of heroes for his dramatic overtime game-winning goal versus Northeastern in the 1987 Beanpot final. He was named the tournament MVP for his efforts that evening. Kelfer crossed the 20-goal plateau in his sophomore, junior, and senior years. He also led the team in scoring in his final two seasons. Kelfer resides in the number nine position on the Terrier all-time list, with 83 goals, 89 assists, and 172 points.

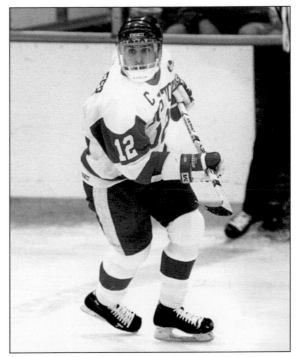

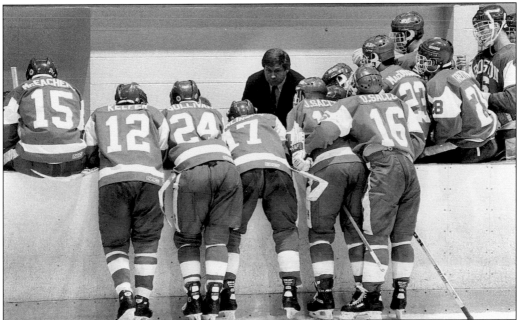

ASSISTANT COACH BEN SMITH. The dry-witted Ben Smith was a Terrier assistant coach and recruiting coordinator for a decade (1981–1990) and a welcome addition to Jack Parker's staff throughout the 1980s. During Smith's tenure, the Terriers won four Beanpots, a Hockey East championship, and played in three NCAA tournaments. The former Harvard Class of 1968 All-Ivy defenseman departed Boston University to become the head coach at Dartmouth and later Northeastern. In 1998, Smith coached the U.S. Women's Olympic Hockey Team to the first ever gold medal in Nagano, Japan.

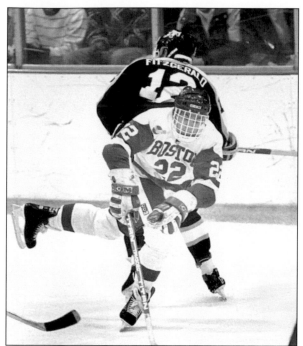

VILLE KENTALA '89. Ville Kentala holds the distinction of being first in a lengthy line of players to cross the Atlantic from Finland to skate for the Terriers. Kentala came to Boston University in 1986, and played three varsity seasons. He scored the first goal on opening night at Boston College's Kelley Rink on November 1, 1988, to open up a 6-3 Boston University victory.

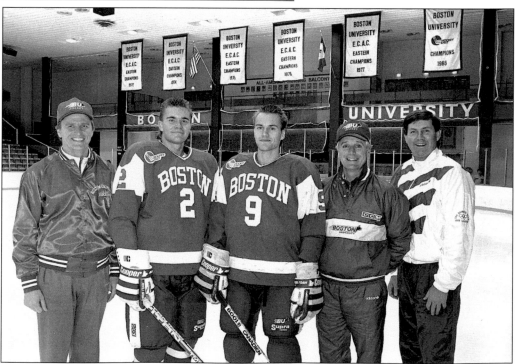

THE BOSTON UNIVERSITY "FINNISH CONNECTION." Several Finnish players followed Kentala's lead in the 1990s. Two of the first were Peter Ahola (2) and Petteri Koskimaki (9), who both arrived in 1989. With them, from left to right, are assistant coach Perti Hasanen, head coach Jack Parker, and assistant coach Ben Smith. Hasanen, a Finnish native, was the man instrumental in recruiting the players from his homeland to Boston University.

Five
Days of Dominance
(1991–2002)

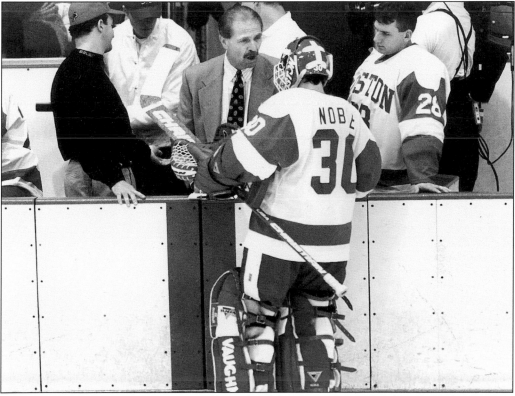

Assistant Coach Bill Berglund. Bill Berglund (center, wearing a tie) came to the Terriers in 1989 to work with the goaltenders. His outstanding record of training net-minders such as Rich Burchill, Tim Marshall, and Bruce Racine at Northeastern continued during an eight-year run with the Terriers. The former original New England Whalers net-minder was a vital factor in the development of Scott Cashman, Tom Noble (foreground) (30), J.P. McKersie, Derek Herlofsky, and Michel Larocque (right) (28)—an impressive list of goalies. The Terriers qualified for the NCAA tournament every year that assistant coach Berglund worked with the team. He went on to become a scout for the Montreal Canadiens. Pictured with Berglund on the bench are current Boston University equipment manager Mike DiMella (left, wearing a dark shirt) and trainer Larry Venis (to the back right of Berglund).

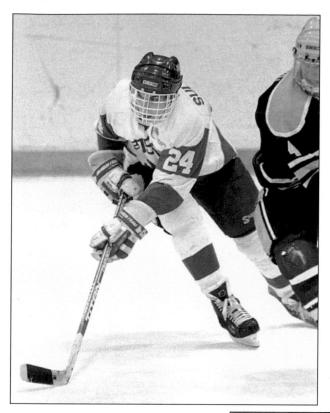

MIKE SULLIVAN '90. The captain of the 1989–1990 team, Mike Sullivan led the Terriers back to the NCAA tournament after a four-year hiatus. Offensively, Sullivan averaged almost one point per game for his career: 61 goals, 77 assists, and 138 points in 141 games. He exceeded any of his statistical achievements with his outstanding leadership ability both on and off the ice, as evidenced by his back-to-back Bennett McInnis Spirit Awards in 1989 and 1990. Sullivan went on to a 12-year professional career with the NHL's Phoenix Coyotes.

JOE SACCO. Joe Sacco was a high school standout from nearby Medford High School. The right wing brought his game to Commonwealth Avenue in 1987. Sacco was a member of the Terriers' "Century Club" (100 or more points) and saw his production improve in each of his three seasons as a Terrier, culminating with a 52-point (24 goals and 28 assists) season in his final year at Boston University. Playing his senior year on a line with Tony Amonte and Shawn McEachern, Sacco played a prominent role in the Terriers' return to the 1990 NCAA championships in Detroit. Sacco has been a regular NHL skater for 12 seasons, including time with the Washington Capitals.

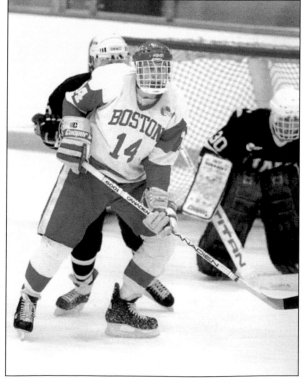

Scott Cashman and Peter Ahola.
Two of the main reasons for the Terriers' turnaround in 1989–1990 were numbers 1 and 2. Goaltender Scott Cashman (1) came to Boston University in the fall of 1989 and quickly made his presence felt. Taking charge of the net-minding position as a freshman, the Kanata, Canada, native was named the team MVP in 1990. Cashman finished his career in 1993 as both the Terrier season (1,027 in 1989–1990) and career (2,478) save leader. Peter Ahola (2) was another in the line of Finnish players to become key contributors to the program. Ahola was a tall, rangy defenseman with excellent all-around skills, and he led the Terrier defensemen in all three offensive categories in 1990–1991: 12 goals, 24 assists, and 36 points. The native of Espoo, Finland, turned professional after his sophomore year and played in the NHL for three seasons before returning to play professionally in his homeland.

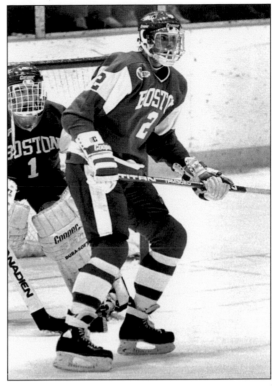

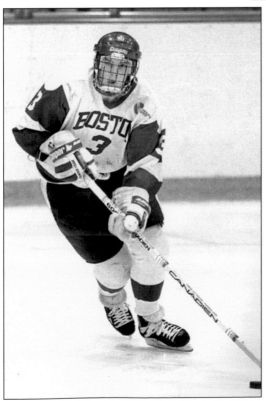

Tony Amonte. Tony Amonte was number three in the Terriers' one-two-three turnaround in 1989–1990. Amonte was explosive on offense, and patrolled the off-wing with an often lethal result for opposing goalies. A recruit from Thayer Academy, he burst onto the college scene with a 25-33-58 rookie season. Despite a mid-season scoring slump in 1990–1991, Amonte finished strong and made good on a promise to his head coach that he would hit the 30-goal mark. His Beanpot MVP performance in 1991 has gone down in history as one of the most memorable individual accomplishments of the tournament. Knocked out on a check by Boston College's Joe Cleary, Amonte responded with a hat trick, and the Terriers defeated the Eagles 8-4. Amonte signed with the New York Rangers after his sophomore year and has been one of the most prolific scorers of the past decade. He is currently the captain of the NHL's Chicago Blackhawks.

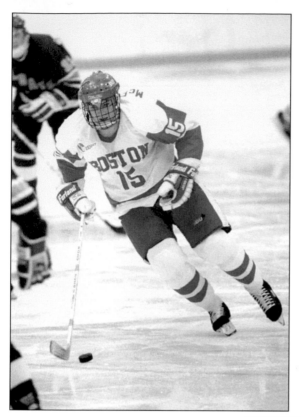

SHAWN MCEACHERN. Shawn McEachern was one of the all-time greatest Massachusetts high school hockey players from Matignon High School. He brought his tremendous speed to the Boston University offensive attack in 1988–1989. McEachern skated with fellow future NHL players Tony Amonte and Joe Sacco in 1989–1990 and then combined with Amonte and freshman Keith Tkachuk in 1990–1991. He saved his best for last and racked up 82 points (34 goals and 48 assists) as a junior in 1991. McEachern's scoring total is second on the Terriers' all-time list, trailing only Jack Garrity (1949–1950). He turned professional after playing for the 1992 U.S. Olympic team in Meribel, France, and has enjoyed a 10-year NHL career, including time with the Ottawa Senators. His overtime dash for the game-winner versus Maine in the 1991 Hockey East championship remains one of the most memorable goals in Terrier hockey annals.

DAVE TOMLINSON '91. Dave "Snipes" Tomlinson is firmly established as one of Boston University's best all-around centers. Tomlinson was a relentless fore-checker, and was often as dangerous when the Terriers were a man down as he was when they were at full strength. His three-on-five short-handed goal in the 1990 Beanpot championship game crushed Harvard and paved the way to a resounding 8-2 Terrier victory. Tomlinson was named the tournament MVP for his superlative effort. Often overshadowed during his final two seasons (1990 and 1991) as the Terriers returned to national prominence, there is no denying his 179 career points, a number seven ranking on the Terrier all-time list. Tomlinson's professional career has taken him to the NHL and to the professional leagues in Europe.

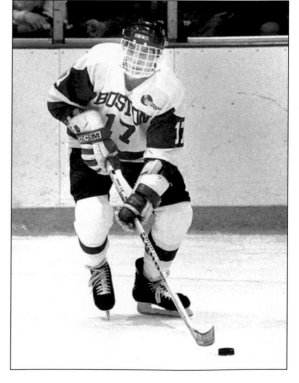

PHIL VON STEFFENELLI '91. Phil
Von Steffenelli was a smooth-skating
defenseman and a key member of
the defensive corps for the Terriers'
back-to-back Beanpot and NCAA
Final Four teams in 1990 and 1991. A
consistent presence in the defensive zone
throughout his career, he stepped up his
offensive contribution dramatically in
his final two seasons with a 15-43-58
scoring line. A corecipient of the Bennett
McInnis Spirit Award as a senior, Von
Steffenelli has gone on to a 10-year
professional career that has included
playing time with the NHL's Ottawa
Senators and Boston Bruins.

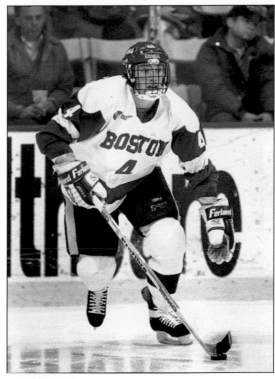

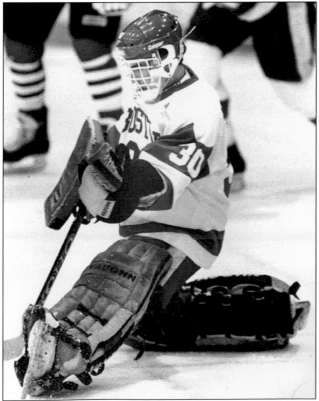

JOHN BRADLEY '91. John Bradley
saved his best for his final season
as a Terrier. As a freshman
"J.B." saw limited action as the
backup goalie to fellow Ocean
State resident Peter Fish. The
following year, Bradley found
himself in a three-man rotation
that also included Bryan LaFort.
In his junior season, Bradley
played sparingly in relief of
Scott Cashman. Then, as a
senior, Bradley split the position
with Cashman and compiled
a 14-4-1 record with a 3.16
goals against average and a
.885 save percentage. His wins
included three shutouts and an
outstanding performance in the
Terriers' 4-3 overtime win over
Maine in the 1991 Hockey East
championship game.

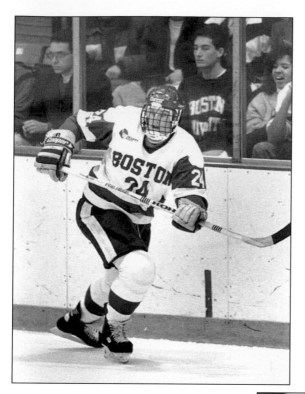

KEITH TKACHUK. Keith Tkachuk brought his power forward game to Boston University in 1990. Tkachuk contributed 17 goals, 23 assists, and 40 points to one of the most prolific scoring lines in Terrier hockey history. He shook off the effects of a knee injury, which severely curtailed his final high school season at Malden Catholic, to become a key member of a Boston University team that advanced to the NCAA title game versus Northern Michigan. Tkachuk has enjoyed a stellar decade-long NHL career, first with the Phoenix Coyotes and then the St. Louis Blues. He also holds the distinction of representing the United States at three Olympics—1992, 1998, and 2002.

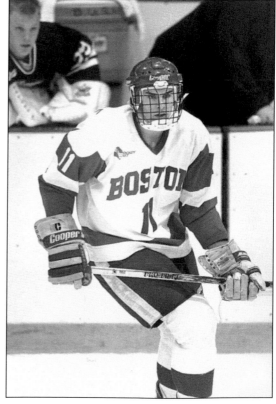

SCOTT LACHANCE. Scott Lachance made a major impact on the 1990–1991 Terrier squad, arguably Boston University's best ever. A highly sought-after recruit out of the Springfield Olympics program, Lachance played with the poise of a veteran from the beginning of his year on Babcock Street. His brilliant diving save positioned David Sacco for the game-tying goal in the Terriers' triple overtime National Championship match with Northern Michigan in St. Paul, Minnesota. A member of the 1992 U.S. Olympic team, Lachance has been a solid defenseman for three NHL clubs during the past decade: the New York Islanders, the Montreal Canadiens, and the Vancouver Canucks.

ED RONAN '91. Ed Ronan defied the odds from the outset of his Terrier career. A relatively unheralded winger from Andover Academy, Ronan, through his persistence and all-out effort, saw his goal production increase from 6 in his first two seasons to 33 his final two. Ronan continued to turn doubters into believers, going on to an NHL career that included a Stanley Cup championship with the 1993 Montreal Canadiens.

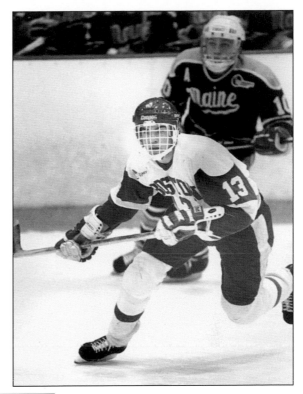

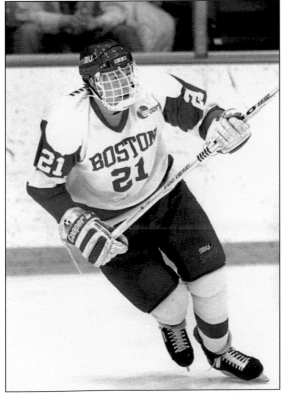

CHRIS MCCANN '91. Chris McCann fulfilled a lifelong dream as a four-year member of the Boston University hockey program. McCann was a high school star in Woburn, Massachusetts, and came to Boston University after a season at Avon Old Farms. His size and physical play made him an important defensive role-player on the Terrier forward lines. McCann had his best offensive year (9-9-18) as a senior. He shared the Bennett McInnis Spirit Award in 1991.

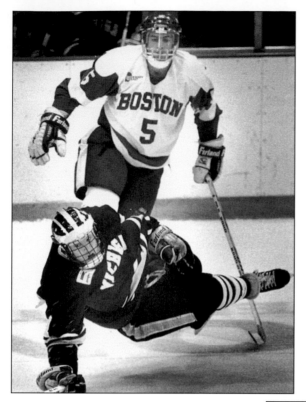

TOM DION '92. Tom Dion grew up in upstate New York, where college hockey is dominated by Clarkson and St. Lawrence. Dion was a solid defender through his first two seasons but suffered a season-ending knee injury his junior year. A healthy return to regular duty on the 1990–1991 team led to captaincy in 1991–1992. In one of only two seasons along with fellow blue-liner Mark Brownschilde, Dion became the steadying influence on a young team that won a third straight Beanpot and also qualified for the NCAA tournament for a third straight year.

KAI LINNA. The line of Finnish defensemen at Boston University begun by Peter Ahola continued with Kai Linna. A member of the National Championship Class of 1995, Linna literally stepped right into Ahola's jersey (number 2) for the 1991–1992 campaign. Linna was an influence in both the offensive and defensive zones throughout his career, and his 7-20-27 scoring totals as a senior were a career best for the 1995 National Champions. His hat trick in the 6-2 NCAA East Regional victory over Lake Superior State made his top offensive performance even more significant. Linna went on to play for the NHL's Nashville Predators.

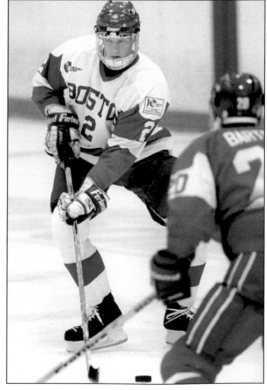

KEVIN O'SULLIVAN. The link between Catholic Memorial and Boston University extends back to head coach Jack Parker. A quarter century after Parker captained the Terriers, Kevin O'Sullivan, a *Boston Globe* All-Scholastic defenseman from Catholic Memorial via Dorchester, Massachusetts, co-captained the Terriers in 1992–1993. O'Sullivan was a regular on the blue line from the time of his arrival for the 1989–1990 season and a member of three Beanpot championship teams. He played in the NCAA tournament for four consecutive years. O'Sullivan skated with several of his high school teammates at Boston University. The Scarlet-Knights-turned-Terriers in the Class of 1993 won 104 games during their four years on Babcock Street.

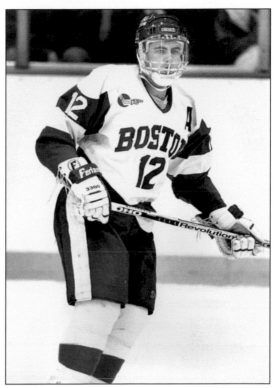

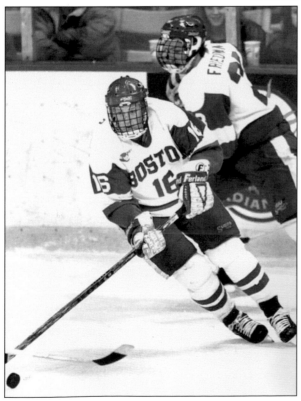

DAVID SACCO '93. David Sacco followed his brother from Medford High School to Boston University in 1988. After a standout rookie season (43 points), a shoulder injury ended his sophomore year after just three games. Back in the potent Terrier lineup in 1990–1991, he finished tied for third in scoring with 60 points. Sacco was a brilliant playmaker, with soft hands and great on-ice vision. He co-captained the Terriers with O'Sullivan in 1992–1993. He completed his illustrious career as Boston University's second all-time leading scorer (217 points) behind John Cullen. He also remains tied with Cullen for first on the Terriers' all-time assist list, with 143. Sacco went on to the 1994 Olympics in Lillehammer, Norway, before playing in the NHL. A chronic shoulder problem prematurely ended his career.

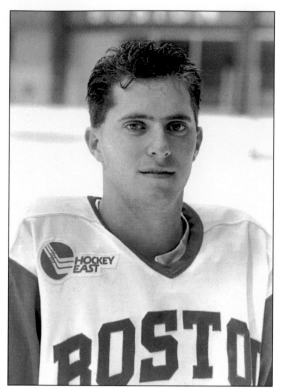

MARK BAVIS '93 AND MIKE BAVIS '93. The Bavis Twins, or "Bavi" as they came to be known, personified the Terriers' team motto: "desire, determination, and the will to win." From their first shift as freshmen to their last as seniors, the twins were a relentless force of nature. Their ability as a penalty-killing tandem was a particularly noteworthy skill. They were honored by the New England Hockey Writers as the best defensive forwards and also shared the Bennett McInnis Spirit Award as both juniors and seniors. Mike (below) is currently a Boston University assistant coach. Mark (left) died tragically on September 11, 2001, aboard United Airlines Flight 175.

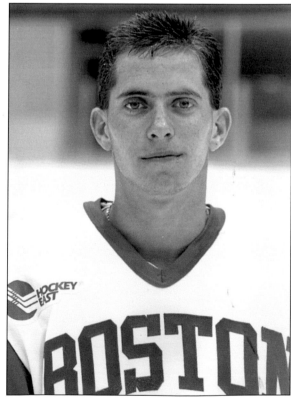

MIKE POMICHTER. Mike Pomichter was a prolific offensive force throughout his three years as a Terrier, and he led the Terriers in goals (28) and scoring (53) in 1993–1994. His 12 tallies on the power play also led the team. Pomichter has played professional hockey since first signing with the Chicago Blackhawks organization in 1994.

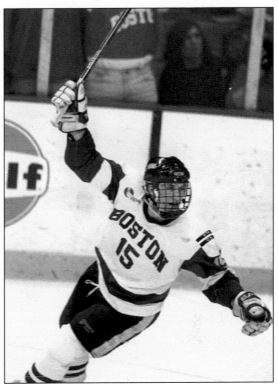

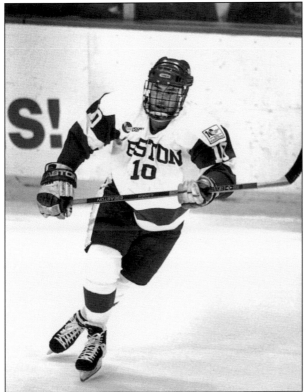

JON JENKINS '94. Jon Jenkins was a transfer from UMass Lowell, and became a vital player for the Terriers from 1992 to 1994. A physical forward with good speed, he spent much of his time as a Terrier on a checking unit with center Jon Pratt and right wing Doug Friedman. Although noted for his ability as a "grinder," Jenkins showed improvement in his offensive game. His 12 goals as a senior marked a career high, none bigger than a key goal in a tense Hockey East quarterfinal series versus Maine at Walter Brown Arena. Jenkins was the Albert Sidd Unsung Hero (Friends of Hockey) Award winner as a senior.

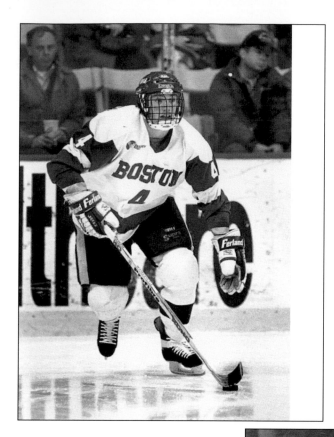

DOUG FRIEDMAN '94. Doug Friedman came to Boston University from Lawrence Academy as an unheralded walk-on with a defined physical side to his game, and he left as the captain of a 34-win team his senior year, the Terriers' most ever wins. Through his first two seasons, Friedman was primarily a checking force on the fourth line. Over his final two years, he registered a record of 26-48-74 and demonstrated a renewed confidence in his offensive skills. Since his graduation from Boston University, Friedman has played professionally for several teams and leagues, including the NHL's Nashville Predators.

RICH BRENNAN '95. Rich Brennan came to Babcock Street from Tabor Academy via Guilderland, New York. Brennan was a New England prep school all-star and had all the requisite skills in his arsenal that any coach would seek if creating a model defenseman. Brennan was an adept puck handler with a booming shot from the point and was equally comfortable thwarting opponents' offensive threats around his own net. He was named the winner of the George V. Brown Award in 1994. Brennan has been a professional since his graduation from the Terriers' 1995 National Championship team, and has played in the NHL for several teams, including the New York Rangers in Wayne Gretzky's final game.

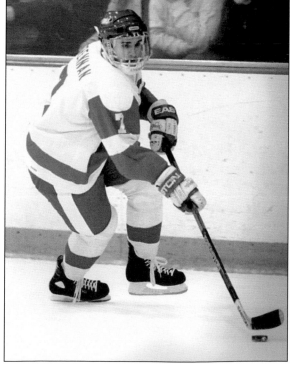

DEREK HERLOFSKY AND J.P. MCKERSIE.
The Terriers recruited two top goaltenders
from the United States Hockey League
in 1991. Derek Herlofsky (right) and J.P.
McKersie (below), from the respective
college hockey–crazed cities of Minneapolis,
Minnesota, and Madison, Wisconsin, left their
roots, journeyed to Boston, and established
themselves as a formidable one-two tandem.
The relatively small Herlofsky relied on his
quickness and athletic ability, while the
imposing McKersie excelled as a more classical
stand-up, angle-playing net-minder. After
sharing time with veteran Scott Cashman
during their first two seasons, Herlofsky and
McKersie settled into a rotation in 1993–1994
for the 34-7 Terriers. The arrangement
looked as if it would stick for the 1994–1995
campaign until a July 1994 accident left
McKenzie in a coma. Remarkably, he came
back to play again for Boston University in
1996 and went on to play professionally.
Herlofsky had the distinction of defeating
his hometown Gophers in the 1995 NCAA
semifinal in Providence, Rhode Island. He
has played professionally on both sides of the
Atlantic in several leagues.

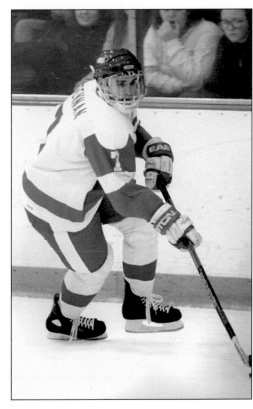

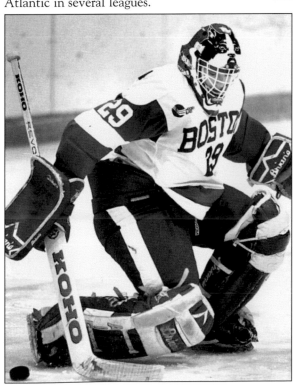

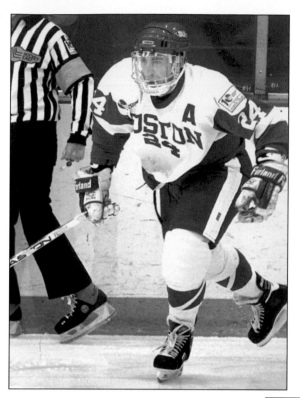

JACQUES JOUBERT '95. The fact that the Terriers had a hockey captain named Jacques Joubert in 1995 was not unusual. The fact that he hailed from college football's most famous address—South Bend, Indiana—was unusual. Joubert's family had Boston area and Notre Dame roots. He had played at the Canterbury School in Connecticut and went on to Princeton. After a transfer to Boston University, Joubert sat out the 1991–1992 season. The following year, he became a key contributor with his goal-scoring skills, sound defensive ethic, and overall hustle. Off the ice, Joubert's intelligent wit and urbane manner always established a positive atmosphere. He was elected team captain for the 1994–1995 season, leading Boston University to its fourth National Championship. He also received the Bennett McInnis Spirit Award in 1994. Joubert's career goal total of 64 ranks him in the Terriers' all-time top 20.

STEVE THORNTON '95. Steve Thornton was a center iceman in a classical old-time hockey way. Thornton was a small guy who could fly and quite simply, with his vision and puck skills, made everybody who surrounded him better. He was a member of the Terriers' National Championship Class of 1995 and became a fixture centering the Terriers' top line. Thornton was a good face-off man and a thorough defensive player in his own end. He shook off the effects of a late-season knee injury, missing just one game. Thornton's 143-point career total ranks him in the Terrier top 20 of all time. He has the distinction of receiving four of the Terriers' major team awards: Most Improved Player (1992), Unsung Hero (1993), Most Valuable Player (1995), and Spirit Award (1995). No individual award could rank with the Terriers' "Triple Crown" (Beanpot, Hockey East, NCAA) accomplishments. A dual citizen (Canada and England), Thornton has played professionally and internationally since his graduation from Boston University.

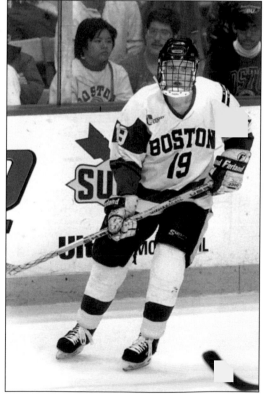

MIKE PRENDERGAST '95. Mike Prendergast lived the local hockey dream. The South Boston native was a consummate sniper for the Catholic Memorial Scarlet Knights, and became an immediate impact Terrier as a freshman, with 19 goals to tie for the team lead. The highlight of Prendergast's rookie season was his Beanpot MVP performance when the Terriers captured their third straight. His best overall offensive year was his last, compiling a record of 17-20-37 for the "Triple Crown" National Champions.

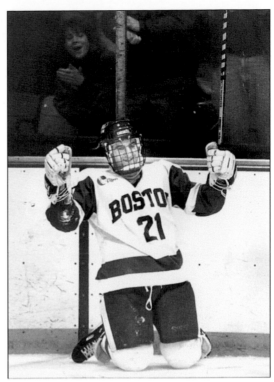

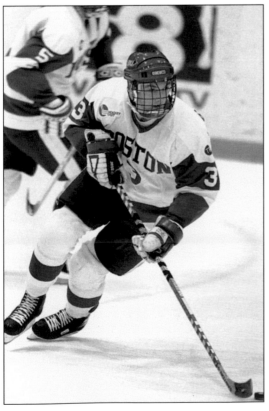

CHRIS O'SULLIVAN. It did not matter what position Chris O'Sullivan played for coach Jack Parker, his skillful hands remained a constant. After a spectacular debut at the Badger Classic Tournament in December 1992, O'Sullivan suffered a serious neck injury that sidelined him for the remainder of the 1992–1993 season. He returned as a defenseman the next year and established him as a Terrier mainstay. O'Sullivan moved to the forward lines in 1994–1995 and had a breakout offensive season (23-33-56) to lead the National Champions in scoring. He played both forward and defense in his final year at Boston University and signed a professional contract with both the Calgary Flames and Anaheim Mighty Ducks. He went on to play in Switzerland. The story of the 11 O'Sullivan children's survival despite losing their father and mother to cancer has been an inspiration to families everywhere.

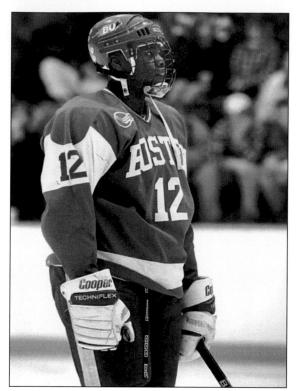

MIKE GRIER. Mike Grier went from prospect to All-American. He began his career at Boston University as an invited walk on and became a poster child for the Terriers' cutting-edge strength and conditioning program under the direction of coach Mike Boyle. Through hard work, Grier made himself a rock-solid linebacker on skates, who gave the term "power forward" a whole new meaning. His promising freshman year goal total of 9 vaulted to a tie for the team lead with 29 the next season as the Terriers ran the tournament tables. Grier departed Boston University after his junior season in 1996 and made history as the first African-American NHL player while skating for the Edmonton Oilers.

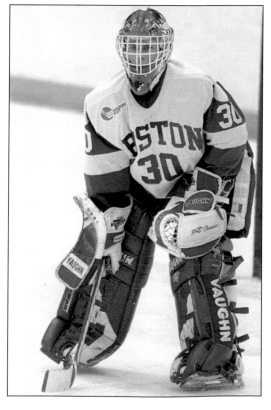

TOM NOBLE '98. Tom Noble saw a number of familiar faces when he entered the Boston University locker room as a freshman. Several of his former Catholic Memorial teammates were already established members of the hallowed Terrier program. The diminutive net-minder was determined to make his own mark. He first split the goaltending chores with Derek Herlofsky and later with Michel Larocque. Noble was the ultimate winner in high school and seemed to be tougher to beat when there was more on the line. Among his 55 career wins was the 1995 National Championship game.

KEN RAUSCH '95. If Ken Rausch had a business card as a Boston University player it would have said, "tournaments a specialty." Rausch was a virtually unknown walk-on from Connecticut who worked his way into the Terrier lineup as a smart, defensive role-player on the forward lines of some explosive Terrier teams. Rausch's overtime game winner against the Minnesota Gophers on their home ice delivered the Terriers to victory on New Year's Eve 1994 at the Mariucci Classic. Rausch's tournament heroics were far from over during the Terriers' National Championship season. His 3-1-4 record garnered the quiet left wing MVP honors in the 1995 Beanpot Tournament, the last one held in the Boston Garden. Rausch is another Terrier who went on to a coaching career. He became the assistant to former Terrier assistant coach Blaise MacDonald (1990–1996) at UMass (Lowell).

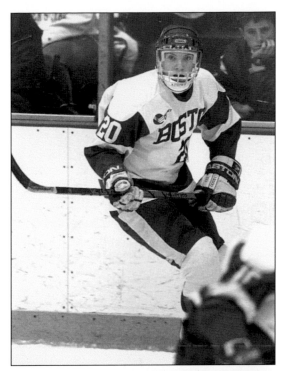

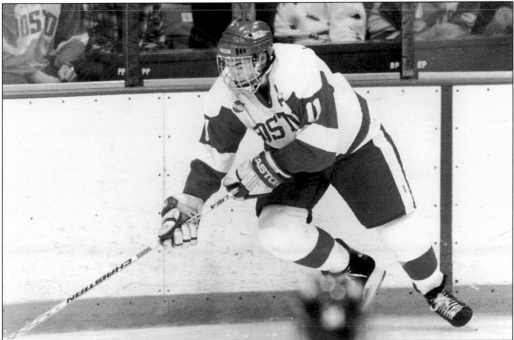

BOBBY LACHANCE '96. Bobby Lachance took his considerable playmaking skills to Boston University from the Springfield Olympics program in 1992. Lachance's 96 career assists rank 13th on the Terriers' all-time list. The younger brother of Boston University defenseman Scott Lachance had his best offensive year as a senior (15-38-53) on the Terriers' explosive 1995–1996 team.

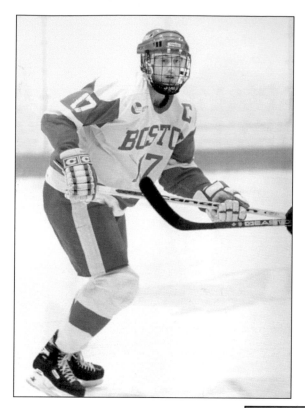

JAY PANDOLFO '96. Jay Pandolfo was the co-captain of the 1995–1996 Terriers. He came back from an injury that limited him during the National Championship run in 1995 to notch 38 goals (third best single-season record of all time). The power forward from Burlington, Massachusetts, was an All-American and Hobey Baker award runner-up in 1996, and he showed a great nose for the net throughout his Terrier career. His 169 points ranks number 11 of all time at Boston University. "Pando" played in the NCAA Final Four in each of his four years, and his Terrier teams compiled a 124-29-8 overall record. He was named to the Boston University Hall of Fame in October 2001. As the Terrier captain in 1996, he will always be remembered for how he kept the team together and handled the difficult aftermath of Travis Roy's tragic accident. He is currently a member of the NHL's New Jersey Devils.

DOUG WOOD '96. When you think of tough-as-nails Terrier defensemen, the name Doug Wood comes to mind very quickly. Wood was a steady defenseman who got the extra power play time and made the most of it. He put up his best offensive numbers as a senior in 1995–1996 with a record of 9-26-35. "Woody" was a highly deserving recipient of the Friends of Hockey Albert Sidd Unsung Hero Award in 1996.

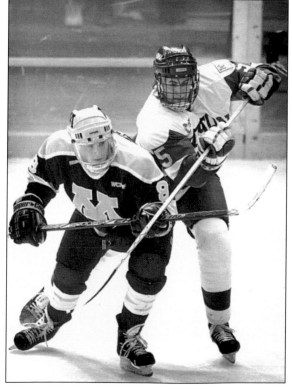

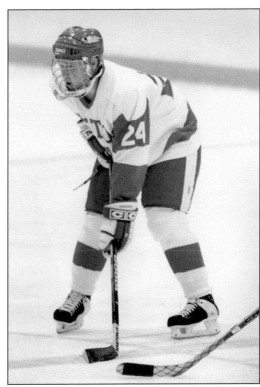

TRAVIS ROY. The star-crossed fate of Travis Roy's Boston University hockey career was played out in a mere 11 seconds. On his first shift in the Terriers' season opener versus North Dakota on October 20, 1995, the Yarmouth, Maine, and former prep all-star at Tabor Academy crashed into the boards and suffered a paralyzing injury. The outpouring of support for Roy and his family in the aftermath of the tragedy was unprecedented. His extraordinary courage was documented in his best-selling book *Eleven Seconds*. Roy went on to get his Boston University degree in communications. He currently resides in Boston and is very active in the fund-raising needed for the research and development relative to a cure for spinal injuries. He is shown (above) in his official Terrier player portrait and on the occasion of the retirement of his number 24 (left) with his parents Lee and Brenda Roy at Walter Brown Arena. He is the only player so honored in Boston University hockey history.

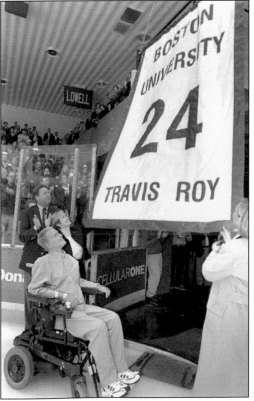

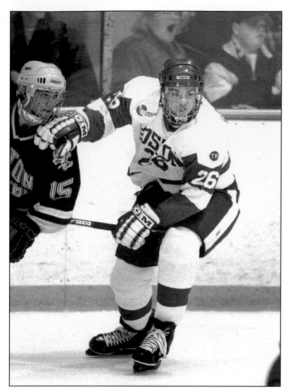

JON COLEMAN '97. Jon Coleman was an effortless skater, as well as a defenseman with solid offensive skills. The former prep star from Andover Academy racked up 96 career assists, ranking him 14th on the Terriers' all-time list and 4th among all defensemen. Coleman played in the NCAA Frozen Four in each of his four years as a Terrier.

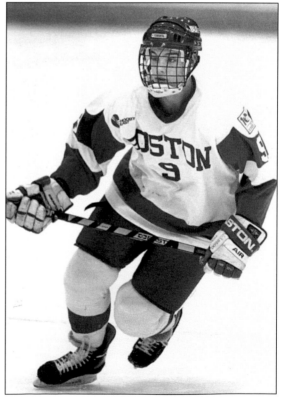

SHAWN BATES '97. Shawn Bates was one of the fastest skaters to ever wear a scarlet-and-white sweater and was another local public high school (Medford) player who proved that the boys from the "publics" can still play. His best season was 1995–1996 in which he earned a 28-22-50 record. His 73 career goals place him 17th all-time. He went on to the NHL to play for the New York Islanders after previously playing for his hometown Boston Bruins.

TOM POTI. Tom Poti's two seasons as a Terrier featured a plethora of needle-threading passes and defender-freezing shifts. The highly skilled offensive-minded defenseman scored 63 points (17-46) in 66 career games. A consummate power play quarterback, he set up Nick Gillis for the overtime Beanpot final winning goal in 1998 versus Harvard University. Poti signed with the NHL's Edmonton Oilers in 1998 but has since taken his act to Broadway as a member of the New York Rangers.

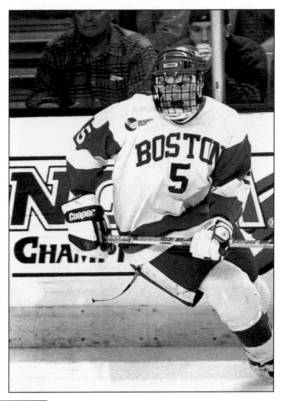

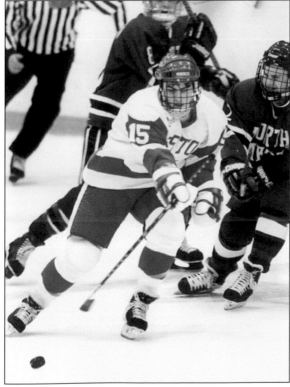

MIKE SYLVIA '98. Mike Sylvia followed the well-traveled path from Catholic Memorial to the Walter Brown Arena. Sylvia was a member of the 1995 National Champions, and his production and contribution increased in each of his four seasons, culminating with a 19-21-40 scoring line in 1997–1998.

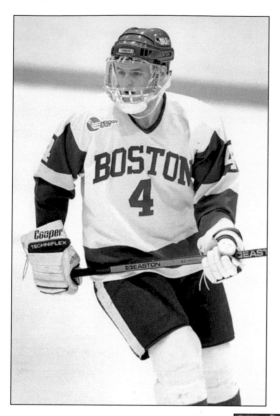

CHRIS KELLEHER '98. The Terrier connection to St. Sebastian's that began with the late Kevin Mutch (1981) was revisited with the arrival of Chris Kelleher for the 1994–1995 season. Kelleher, who had played for assistant coach Mutch at St. Sebastian's in 1992, fulfilled his dream of becoming a Terrier. A blue liner with size and good puck-handling skills, he racked up an impressive 14-51-65 line his final two seasons at Boston University. Kelleher was co-captain of the 1997–1998 team, and he later got an opportunity to play for the Boston Bruins.

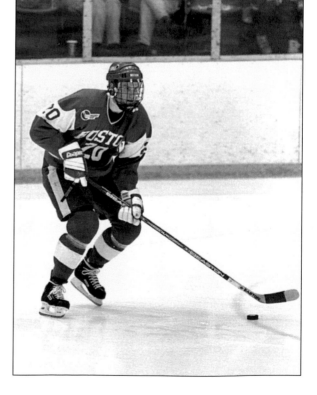

JEFF KEALTY '98. Defenseman Jeff Kealty had to deal with the pressure of a high draft selection early in his Boston University career. Once he placed the expectations behind him, Kealty settled down and finished his Terrier career with two solid seasons, leading all Terrier defensemen in goals his senior year. With his playing career ended by a neck injury, he became a scout for the NHL's Nashville Predators.

CHRIS DRURY '98. Chris Drury is one of the most-honored players in Boston University hockey history. A two-time All-American (1997 and 1998) and Hobey Baker Award winner (1998) as college hockey's most outstanding player, Drury went from Most Improved Player (1996) to two-time team MVP (1997 and 1998) and two-time winner of the Walter Brown Award (1997 and 1998) as the top American-born player in New England. He played on four consecutive Beanpot championship teams and in four straight NCAA tournaments. He was named Beanpot MVP in 1996 and Hockey East tournament MVP in 1996 as the Terriers defeated the University of New Hampshire 4-2 for the title. His overtime goal versus Denver at the 1997 East Regional delivered the Terriers to the Frozen Four in Milwaukee and a memorable victory over the University of Michigan, the defending national champions. Drury won the Calder Trophy as NHL Rookie of the Year in 1999. He has continued his winning ways as a prominent member and assistant captain of the Colorado Avalanche, the 2001 Stanley Cup champions.

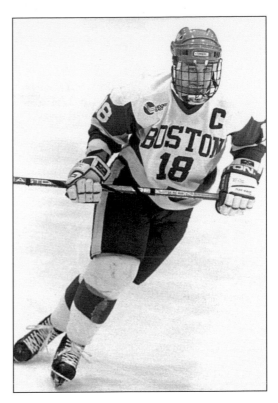

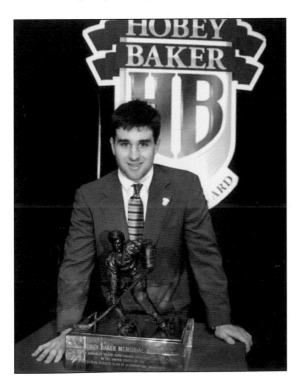

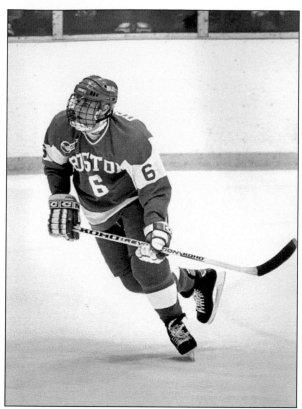

ALBIE O'CONNELL '99 AND CARL CORRAZZINI '99. The line of captaincy at Boston University tracing back to St. Sebastian's was extended further in 1999 and 2001. Albie O'Connell captained and led the 1998–1999 team to a fifth straight Beanpot championship. O'Connell's 39 points (9-30) led the team in scoring. Carl Corrazzini picked up the St. Sebastian's–Boston University captain baton in 2000–2001. The speedy Corrazzini, shown here racing past a Maine defender, seemed to save his best for the Black Bears. He was named Maine's "most honored opponent" in 2000. Corrazzini led the 1999–2000 team in goals (22) and the 2000–2001 team in scoring, with 36 points.

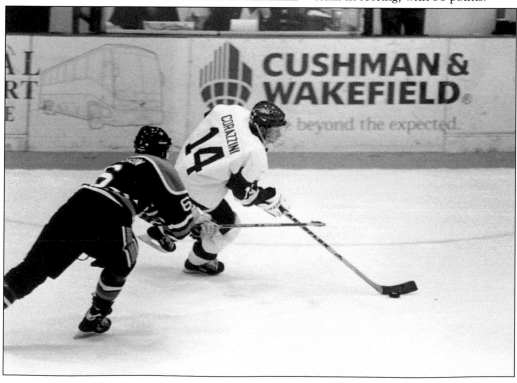

"Deger and Hero." It could have
been the name of an action movie.
As the captain of the 1999–2000
team, Tommi Degerman '00 (right)
did an exemplary job assisted by
his roommate and close friend
Chris Heron '00 (below). The first
European captain of the Terriers from
Helsinki, Finland, Degerman and
Ontario native Heron fittingly tied
for the top in Terrier scoring, each
with 43 points. The 2000 team won
a record-extending sixth Beanpot
championship, defeating Boston
College 4-1. In the NCAA East
Regional in Albany, New York, the
Terriers' hearts were broken in an epic
four overtime loss to St. Lawrence
(3-2). "We died with our boots on,"
was the memorable postgame quote
from captain Degerman, a former
sergeant in the Finnish army.

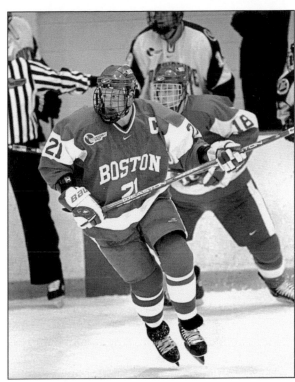

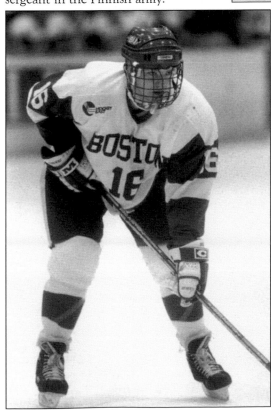

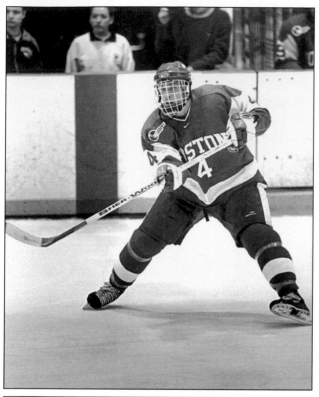

CHRIS DYMENT '02 AND MIKE PANDOLFO '02. For the first time in four years, the Terrier program selected co-captains for the 2000–2001 campaign. It turned out to be a fortuitous choice. Defensemen Chris Dyment (Reading, Massachusetts) and Mike Pandolfo (Burlington, Massachusetts, via St. Sebastian's), a couple of local skaters, led the Terriers back from a disappointing campaign the previous year. Dyment anchored the Terrier defensive corps and posted a record of 7-17-24, while Pandolfo led the team in goals (22) and scoring (40 points) as the Terriers recaptured the Beanpot and returned to the NCAA tournament, finishing with a 25-10-3 record.

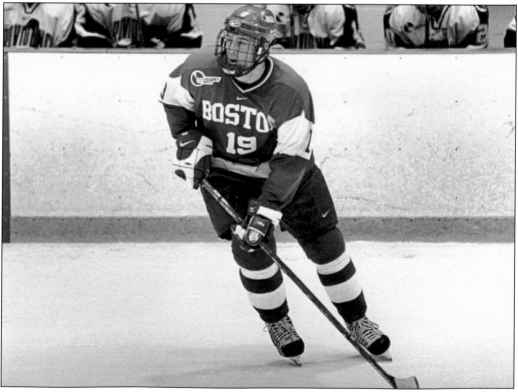

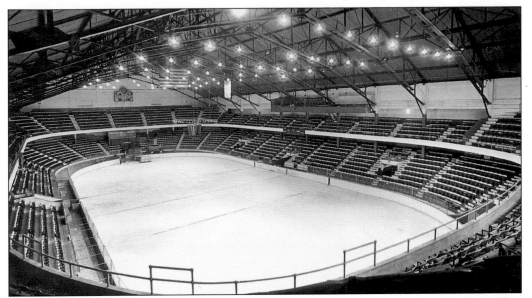

BOSTON ARENA, HOME OF THE TERRIERS FROM 1917 TO 1971. Boston Arena, the oldest continuously operating indoor ice arena in North America (since 1910), was the original home of the Terriers, and just about everybody else on skates in the Greater Boston area, from the program's inception in 1917 through the 1970–1971 season. The Terriers' overall record was 306-158-11, for a .616 winning percentage.

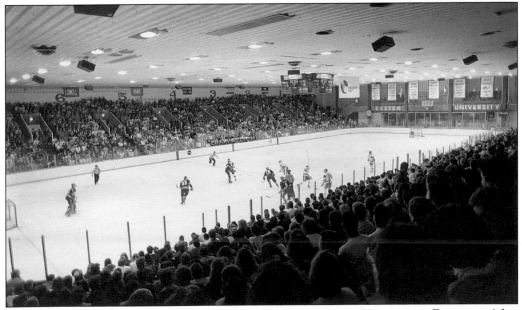

THE WALTER BROWN ARENA, HOME OF THE TERRIERS FROM 1971 TO THE PRESENT. After many years of debate and delay, the Terriers finally had a home of their own for the 1971–1972 season. The Walter Brown Arena has been the stage for countless great moments in Terrier history. The raucous barn on Babcock Street has afforded Boston University quite a home-ice advantage as evidenced by their overall record of 338-116-33 (.728). There is a new home for Terrier hockey on the horizon. The Armory project includes a state-of-the-art 5,800 seat hockey arena. The Terriers are scheduled to make the move for the 2004–2005 season.

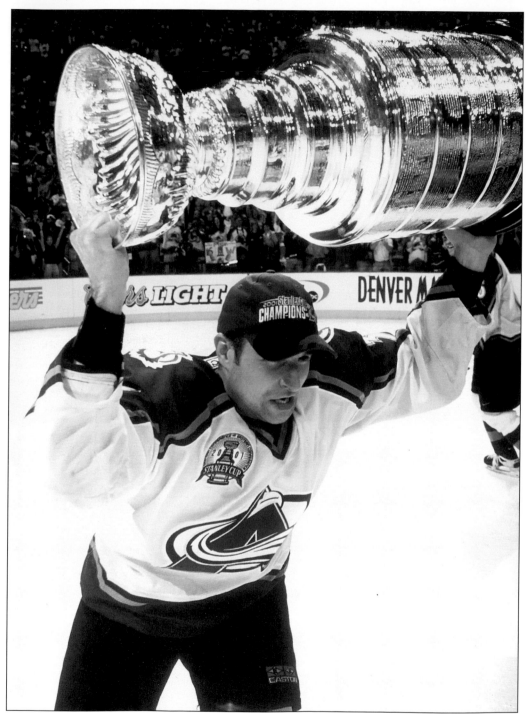

CHRIS DRURY '98 WITH THE STANLEY CUP. Chris Drury climbed yet another mountain in 2001. A Little League World Series champion (1989) and an NCAA champion (1995), Drury added Stanley Cup champion to his resume of outstanding achievements in June 2001. As a member of the NHL's Colorado Avalanche, the 1999 Calder Trophy winner as rookie of the year has scored more playoff goals (25) than any active player since coming into the league.

Six

TERRIER TOURNAMENT TRIUMPHS

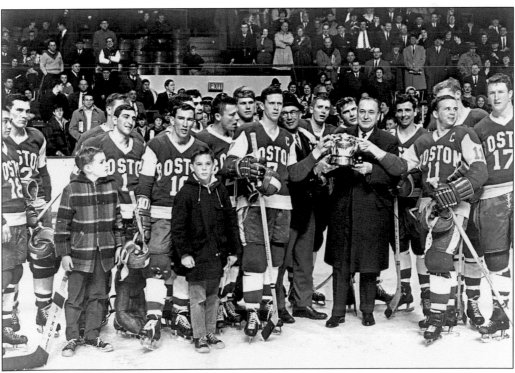

THE 1967 BEANPOT CHAMPIONS. The Terriers celebrate their first ever back-to-back Beanpot championship. The Terriers defeated Harvard University 8-3 in an opening-round match before shutting out Northeastern University 4-0 for the title. Co-captains Jim Quinn (7) and Peter McLachlan (11) pose with Boston Garden president Eddie Powers (wearing a tie and an overcoat), coach Jack Kelley (wearing a hat), future captain and coach Jack Parker (to the back right of Kelley), and Kelley's sons (left foreground), one of whom, today, is television producer David E. Kelley.

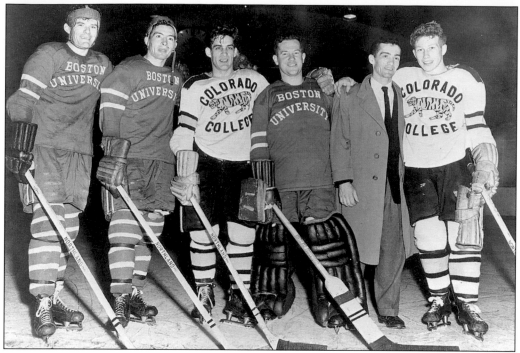

THE 1950 NCAA ALL-TOURNAMENT TEAM. The Terriers were defeated in the 1950 NCAA championship game by Colorado College but were still able to place three members on the All-Tournament team. The are, from left to right, Boston University forward Jack Garrity, Boston University forward Walter Anderson, Colorado College defenseman Jim Starruk, Boston University goalie Ike Bevins, Michigan defenseman Ross Smith, and Colorado College forward and former Cambridge Rindge Technical School star Tony Frasca.

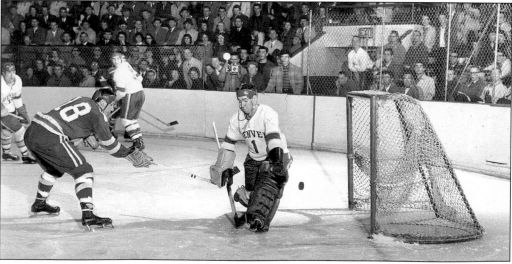

THE 1960 NCAA TOURNAMENT. The Terriers returned to the NCAA tournament for the first time in seven years in 1960. Playing on their home ice at Boston Arena, Boston University lost to eventual champion Denver 6-4 in the semifinal before beating St. Lawrence in the consolation game 7-6, for a third place finish. Boston University forward Bill McCormack (18) bursts in to shoot on the Pioneer goal.

THE 1966 BEANPOT. The 1966 Beanpot championship was the first for Terrier head coach Jack Kelley and began a remarkable Boston University run of 23 titles in 37 years, which dates to the present day. Captain Dennis O'Connell holds the coveted trophy with an elated coach Jack Kelley.

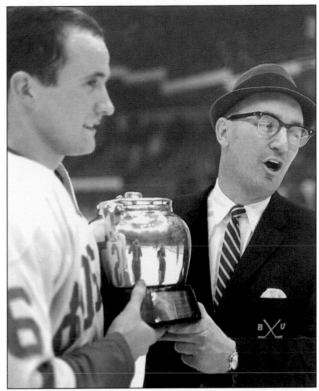

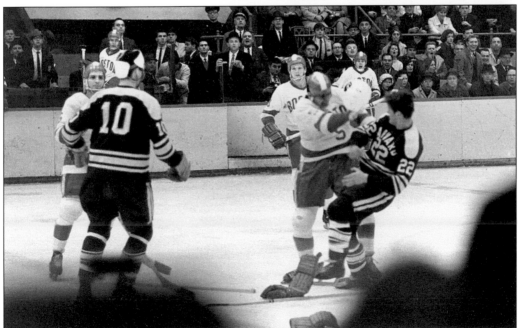

THE 1966 BEANPOT BRAWL. With the end result determined early in what became a 9-2 Boston University title game triumph over Harvard, the on-ice proceedings got out of hand. Boston University forward Fred Bassi (5) uncorks a right jab to deck Harvard forward Montague "Tag" Demment (22) as players and fans alike look on in amazement.

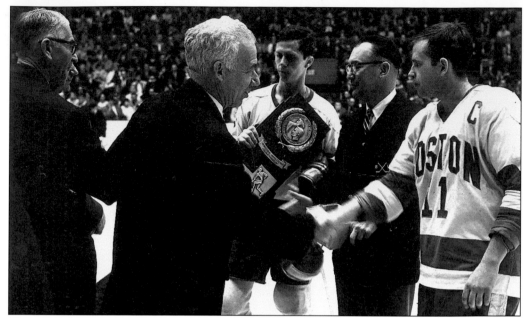

THE 1967 NCAA RUNNERS-UP (MINNEAPOLIS, MINNESOTA). The 1967 Terriers won a second consecutive Beanpot. In both the ECAC and NCAA tournaments, Boston University was runner-up to Cornell University, defeated in the two championship games by the Big Red and goaltender Ken Dryden by scores of 4-3 and 4-1 respectively. Co-captains Jim Quinn and Peter McLachlan (11) flank head coach Jack Kelley accepting the NCAA second-place trophy.

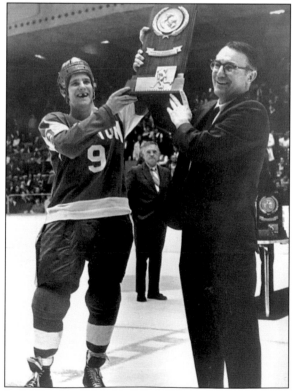

CAPTAIN STIRLING AND COACH KELLEY ACCEPT THE 1971 NCAA TROPHY. The NCAA story had a different ending four years later when the Terriers' next trip to the national tournament in Syracuse, New York, produced victories over Denver and Minnesota by identical 4-2 scores—and the first Boston University national championship. Four Terriers received All-Tournament team recognition: defenseman Bob Brown, forward Donald Cahoon, goalie Dan Brady (Most Outstanding Player), and forward Steve Stirling (left), the team captain, pictured here with coach Jack Kelley. The 1970–1971 team was one of college hockey's greatest, compiling a 28-2-1 record.

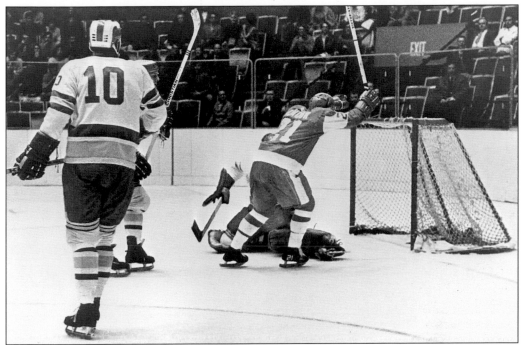

NCAA Action versus Denver, 1971. Left wing Donald Cahoon celebrates one of his two goals in the Terriers' semifinal victory over Denver. Cahoon was named to the All-Tournament team.

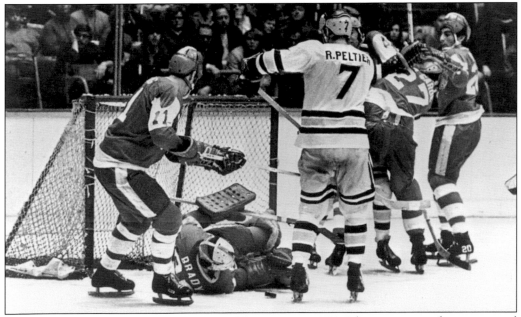

NCAA Action Versus University of Minnesota, 1971. The action gets hectic around the Terrier net in the 1971 championship game versus Minnesota. Forward Wayne Gowing (11) comes back to help out defensemen Mike Lagarde (27) and Bob Murray (20) (far left). A sliding Dan Brady makes one of his 30 saves. The junior goalie was named the tournament's Most Outstanding Player.

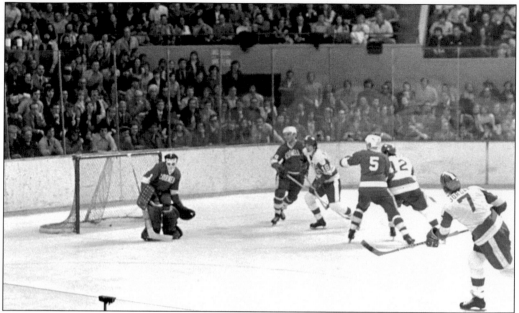

NCAA Action Versus Cornell University in the Title Game, 1972. The Terriers completed their "Triple Crown" 1971–1972 season with a third title (Beanpot, ECAC, and NCAA) captured on Boston Garden ice. All-American defenseman Ric Jordan (7) blasts a slap shot toward Cornell net-minder Dave Ellenbass. Boston University forwards Guy Burrowes (16) and John Danby (12) battle the Cornell defense for position in front of the cage.

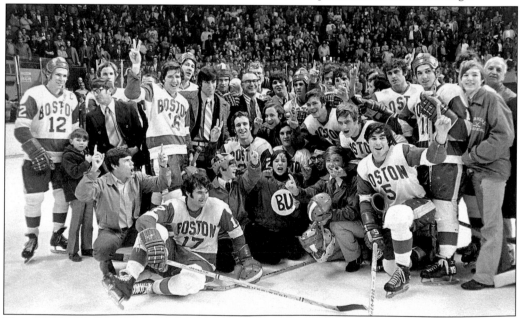

The 1972 NCAA Celebration. It has now been three decades since any college hockey team has accomplished the feat these jubilant Terriers completed. The 1971–1972 team gathers for this group victory portrait. A 4-0 mastery of archrival Cornell University provided a measure of revenge for Terrier fans who remembered the 1967 title-game loss to Cornell in Minneapolis, Minnesota.

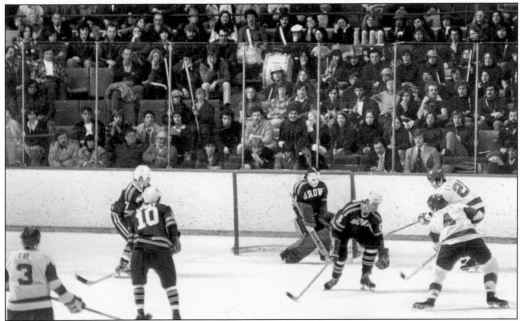

DOMINATING THE ECAC TOURNAMENT. Perhaps the best of the four championship squads was the 1975–1976 team. After surviving a wide-open quarterfinal match with Commonwealth Avenue neighbor Boston College (6-5), Boston University went on to handle Harvard University (8-4) in the semifinal and overwhelm Brown University (9-2) in the final. Here Mike Eruzione (21) looks to follow up a power-play bid by Mike Fidler (4) on Brown net-minder Kevin McCabe. Point man Gary Fay (3) closes in to survey the flurry around the Brown cage. Jack Parker (below), flanked to the left by his co-captain Peter Brown, holds the tournament hardware.

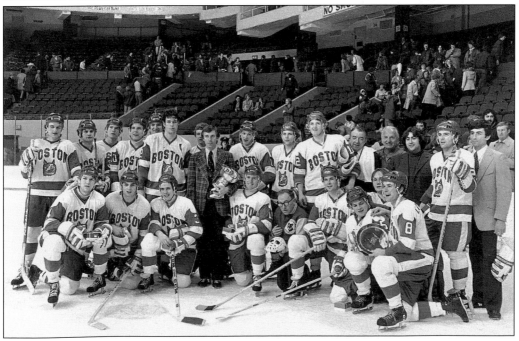

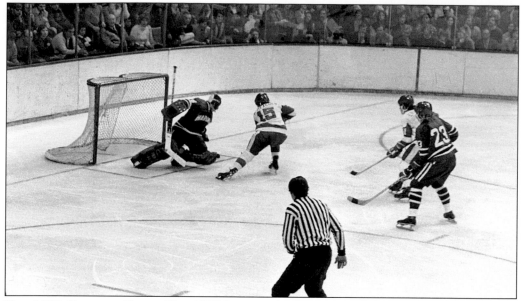

THE 1975 BEANPOT FINAL. The 1975 Beanpot final was one of the Terriers' all-time great big-game performances. Boston University (the East's number two ranked team) faced Harvard University (ranked first), a team that had humbled them by a 7-2 score in December. As has so often been the case, February's second Monday proved to be a different story. The Terriers turned the tables with a resounding 7-2 victory of their own for the Beanpot championship. Three-time All-American Rick Meagher (15) dekes to the backhand on Harvard goalie Brian Petrovek as left wing Mike Eruzione (21), the Terriers' fourth all-time leading scorer, goes to the net.

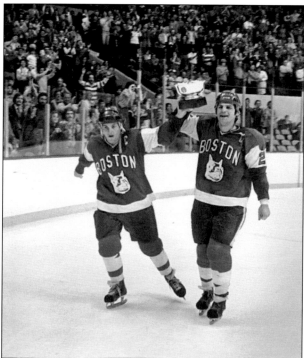

THE 1977 ECAC FINAL. The 1976–1977 Terrier hockey team featured Rick Meagher (left) and Mike Eruzione (right) as the team co-captains. Here, the inseparable duo takes a victory lap at the Boston Garden, holding aloft the ECAC trophy earned by virtue of an 8-6 victory over the University of New Hampshire. It was the fourth consecutive title for Boston University.

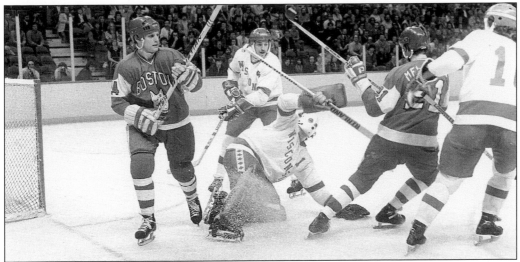

THE 1978 NCAA SEMIFINAL VERSUS WISCONSIN. The 1978 Terriers squeaked by New Hampshire 6-5 in overtime in the ECAC quarterfinals only to be upset by Providence College in a semifinal game. After a consolation game victory over Cornell University, the 26-2 Terriers were granted a second opportunity to qualify for the NCAA final four. A victory at Providence (5-3) in a rematch of the ECAC semifinal brought the Terriers back to Rhode Island for an NCAA semifinal date with powerful University of Wisconsin. Terrier forwards Todd Johnson (24) and John Melanson (21) played key defensive roles in the 5-2 victory. Johnson, a freshman from Wayland, Massachusetts, spent most of the night neutralizing Wisconsin's spectacular center Mark Johnson, future hero of the 1980 Olympic team.

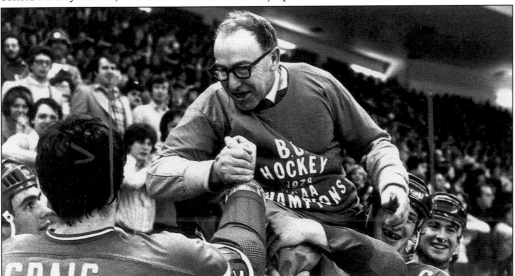

CARL JAMES IN THE 1978 NCAA CELEBRATION. Legendary Boston University equipment manager Carl James plays a familiar role in the middle of the action as the Terriers' 1978 title celebration begins at the Providence Civic Center. Jones, hoisted on the shoulders of the Boston University skaters, congratulates goalie Jim Craig. A former army sergeant, James came to Boston University and became the hockey equipment manager for the next quarter century. A surrogate father and beloved confidante to a generation of Boston University hockey players, the feisty James passed away after a bout with cancer in 1992.

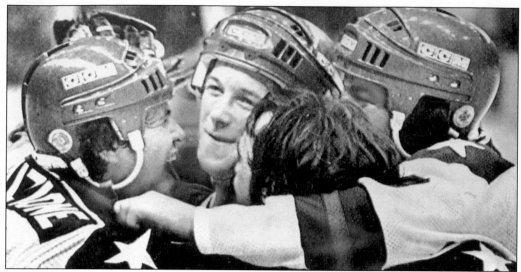

THE "BU FOUR." Before Lake Placid and the 1980 Winter Olympics, they were, from left to right, Mike Eruzione, Jack O'Callahan, Jim Craig, and Dave Silk. After the country's improbable "miracle on ice" gold medal victory, they became known as the "BU Four," forever linked by the historic events that took place in the Adirondacks. On a roster predominated by players from the University of Minnesota and other assorted western colleges, the four Terrier Olympians proudly carried the banner for their school and all of eastern hockey. Craig's spectacular goaltending, Silk's solid all-around play at right wing, O'Callahan's courageous defensive contribution despite a knee injury, and Eruzione's "shot heard 'round the world" game-winning goal versus the Soviet Union, factored prominently in the Americans' golden run to glory. Eruzione, whose name means eruption in Italian, lived up to his name with his memorable marker.

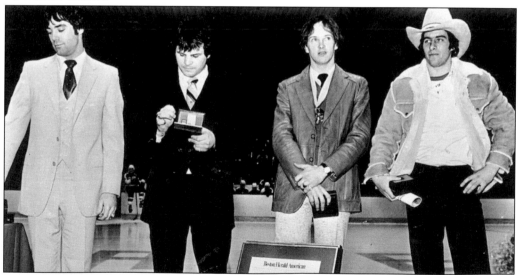

THE OLYMPIANS HONORED AT WALTER BROWN ARENA. Back on campus, the conquering heroes of Lake Placid were feted before the Boston University-Rensselaer Polytechnic Institute game in February. From left to right are goalie Jim Craig, right wing Mike Eruzione, defenseman Jack O'Callahan, and left wing Dave Silk proudly displaying their gold medals amidst additional accolades presented by the university.

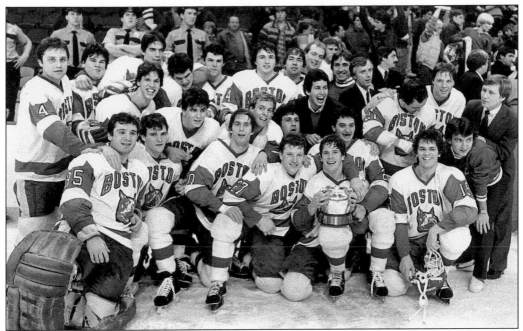

THE 1982 BEANPOT CELEBRATION. The Terriers had endured a couple of uncharacteristic disappointing seasons to begin the 1980s. A resurgent Terrier team put together two memorable February Mondays. In the Beanpot opening round, Boston University breezed past Harvard (5-1). A heavy underdog in the finals, Boston University, led by center Tom O'Regan's (two goals) MVP performance and goalie Cleon Daskalakis (40 saves), the Terriers defeated archrival Boston College 3-1 for the 1982 title. An elated group of Terriers gather around captain Paul Fenton, holding the coveted mug.

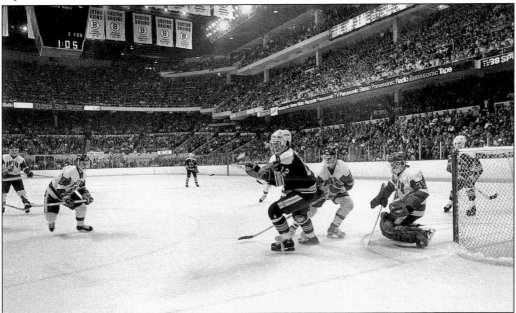

THE 1982 BEANPOT FINAL ACTION. Boston University net-minder Cleon Daskalakis makes one of his 40 saves as Boston College captain Bill O'Dwyer hovers around the net.

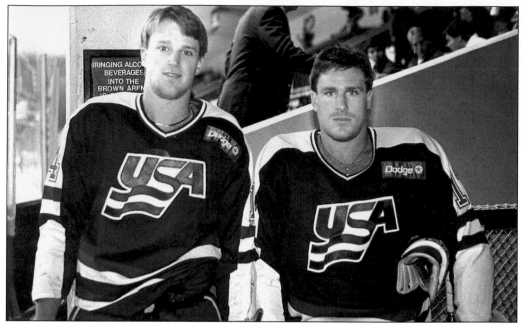

TERRIER OLYMPIANS SCOTT YOUNG AND CLARK DONATELLI. The Terriers' Olympic tradition dates back to 1936, when Boston University Hall of Famers Johnny Lax and Paul Rowe played for the United States at Garmisch-Portenkuden, Germany. Terrier skaters Scott Young (left) and Clark Donatelli (right) were teammates on both the 1988 and 1992 Olympic squads, with Donatelli captaining the 1992 team. Young, currently playing with the NHL's St. Louis Blues, recently played in his third Olympic games at Salt Lake City for the U.S. silver medalists.

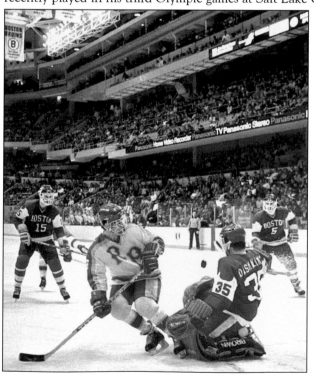

THE 1984 ECAC TITLE GAME. The last ECAC title game before the league divided into ECAC/Hockey East Association was played at the Boston Garden in March 1984. Rensselaer Polytechnic Institute won its first of back-to-back ECAC titles, defeating Boston University in the championship game 5-2. The Engineers challenge Boston University All-American net-minder Cleon Daskalakis as Mark Pierog (15) and Joe Delaney (5) hustle back to help out.

THE 1990 BEANPOT CELEBRATION.
After coming up potless for the
two years closing the 1980s (1988
and 1989), the Terriers surged
back to dominance in the 1990s.
Captain Mike Sullivan holds the
Beanpot aloft as he skates his
victory lap, flanked by Shawn
McEachern (left) and John
Bradley (right). The Terriers'
performance was an impressive one,
defeating their opponents Boston
College (4-3) and Harvard (8-2)
by a combined score of 12-5.

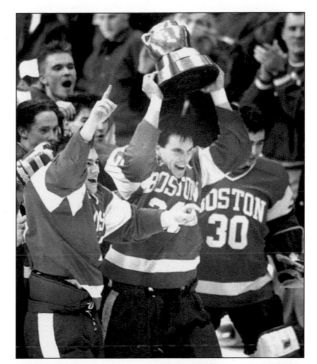

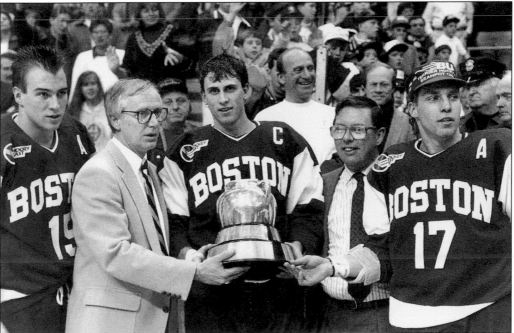

THE 1991 BEANPOT CELEBRATION. The 1990–1991 Terriers captured their second of three straight Beanpots by overwhelming the field. An 8-2 opening round blowout of Harvard was followed by an 8-4 championship game victory over Boston College. In the final, Tony Amonte's rapid-fire hat trick (three goals in 5 minutes and 24 seconds) broke the game open. From left to right are assistant captain Shawn McEachern, head coach Jack Parker, captain Mark Krys, tournament director Steve Nazro, and assistant captain Dave Tomlinson.

121

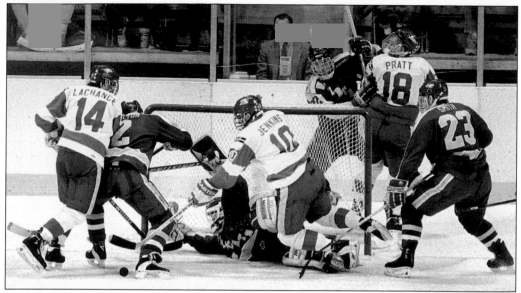

THE NCAA EAST REGIONAL VERSUS NORTHERN MICHIGAN. The 1993 NCAA quarterfinal game at the East Regional (Worcester Centrum) allowed the Terriers to gain a measure of revenge for their heartbreaking triple overtime loss in the 1991 NCAA championship game. The Terriers defeated Northern Michigan 4-1 to advance to the NCAA championships in Milwaukee, Wisconsin. Bob Lachance (14), John Jenkins (10), and John Pratt (18) are shown wreaking some havoc in the Wildcat zone.

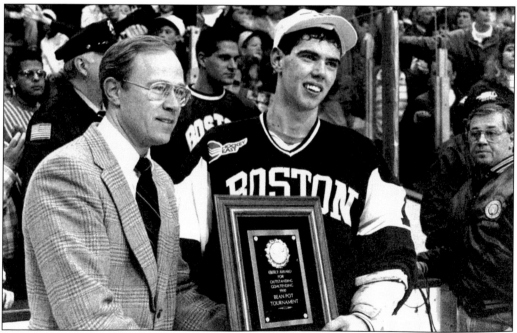

SCOTT CASHMAN ACCEPTING THE EBERLY AWARD. Scott Cashman attended the 1989 Beanpot on his recruiting trip and said, "I can win this thing." Cashman became the only net-minder in tournament history to win the Eberly Award for outstanding goaltending three times—1990, 1991, and 1992. Former Northeastern University goalie Dan Eberly presents Cashman with the 1990 award.

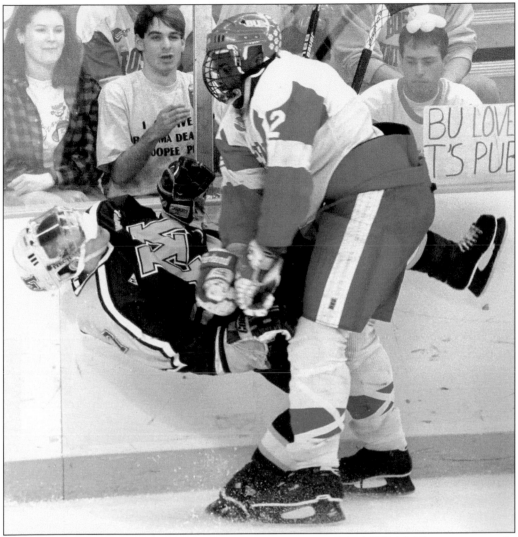

Mike Grier versus the University of Minnesota in the 1995 NCAA Tournament. At 6 feet 2 inches and 237 pounds, Mike Grier resembled a linebacker on skates—and hit like one. This bone-jarring check on a Minnesota player in the 1995 NCAA semifinals at Providence, Rhode Island, sent this Gopher from vertical to horizontal.

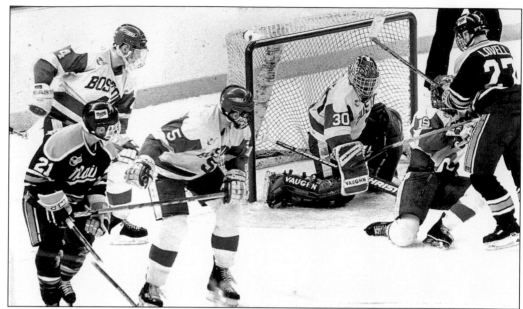

THE 1995 NCAA FINAL VERSUS UNIVERSITY OF MAINE. The calendar may have read April 1, but the Terriers were far from fooled in the 1995 NCAA championship game. After being defeated in both agonizing (8-7 triple overtime versus Northern Michigan in 1991) and humbling (9-1 versus Lake Superior State in 1994) fashion in their two previous title-game appearances, the dogs had their day at Providence Civic Center. A decisive 6-2 win over Maine featured many heroes, including freshman goalie Tom Noble (20 saves), shown turning aside a Black Bear shot as he gets help from defensemen Chris Kelleher (4) and Doug Wood (5) along with center Steve Thornton (19) against Maine forwards Dan Shermerhorn (21) and Tim Lovell (27). On the offensive side, Chris O'Sullivan (3), the tournament's Most Outstanding Player, drives a shot past Maine goalie Blair Allison as Black Bears Jamie Thompson and Chris Imes (4) look on with Boston University's Mike Grier (12).

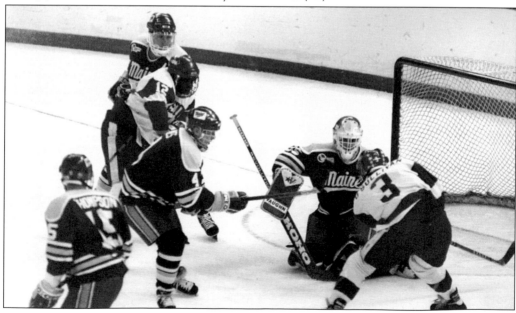

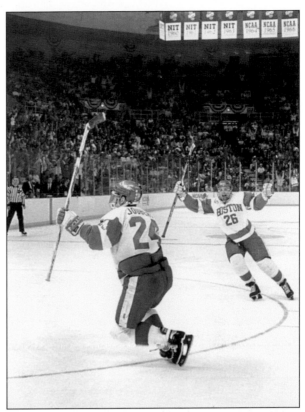

MORE FROM PROVIDENCE. Terrier captain Jacques Joubert (24) celebrates his goal with defenseman Jon Coleman (26) ready to join him. To the victors belong the spoils and the photo opportunities. Terrier seniors, from left to right, Kai Linna, Ken Rausch, Derek Herlofsky, Steve Thornton, Rich Brennan, and Mike Prendergast gather on the mound at Fenway Park before Prendergast does the honors of throwing out the ceremonial first pitch at the Red Sox opening day.

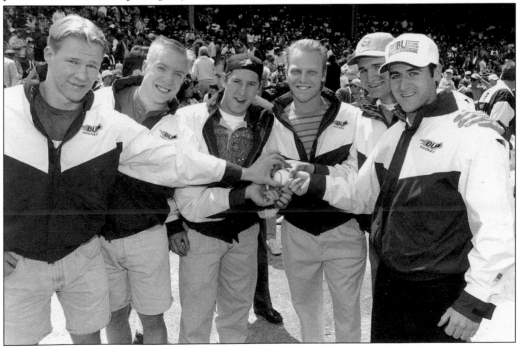

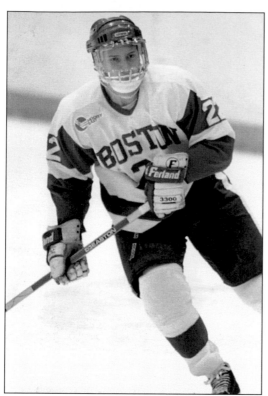

MATT WRIGHT '97. Terrier right wing Matt Wright had the distinction of scoring the final goal in the Beanpot's Boston Garden history. In a 5-1 championship victory over Boston College, Wright provided the exclamation point, thus becoming the answer to a college hockey trivia question.

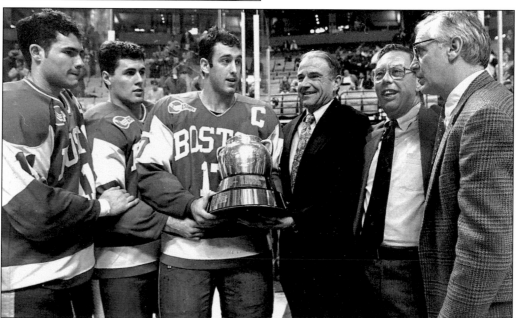

THE 1996 BEANPOT. The new venue (Fleet Center) did not affect the Terriers' performance in 1996. A second straight Beanpot championship was accomplished in a dominant effort. The 11-4 win over Northeastern University resulted in this award-winning score as, from left to right, Terriers' assistant captains Bob Lachance and Doug Wood join captain Jay Pandolfo for the presentation.

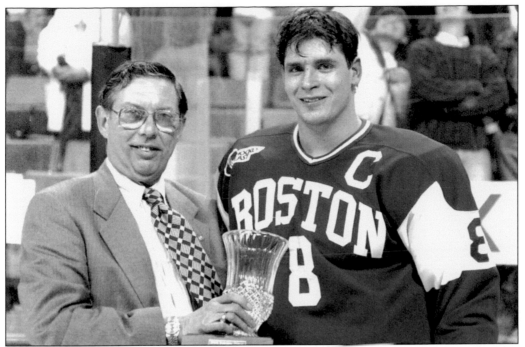

The 1997 Beanpot MVP, Billy Pierce '97. Terrier captain Billy Pierce (right) is all smiles in the aftermath of the 1997 Beanpot championship game. A stirring 4-1 championship victory over archrival Boston College was highlighted by Pierce's game-winning wrist shot high over the glove of Boston College net-minder Gregg Taylor. For his efforts Pierce was presented the MVP award by tournament director Steve Nazro.

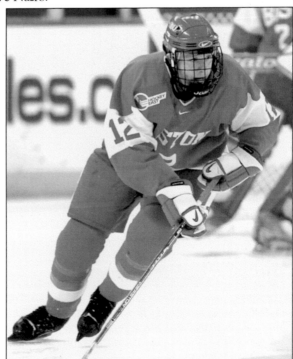

Nick Gillis '01. As a freshman playing in his first Beanpot final in 1998, Nick Gillis exhibited a flair for the dramatic. His reroute of a brilliant pass from MVP Tom Poti resulted in a 2-1 Terrier overtime victory over Harvard—quite a thrill for the local lad from Winthrop.

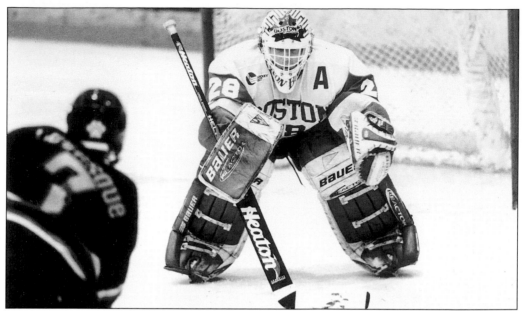

MICHEL LAROCQUE '99. Michel Larocque simply walled up the Terrier net in the 1999 Beanpot final. An underdog Terrier team rode the spectacular 36-save performance by Larocque to a 4-2 win over Northeastern University. The triumph was the Terriers' record-setting fifth straight Beanpot. Larocque was named tournament MVP.

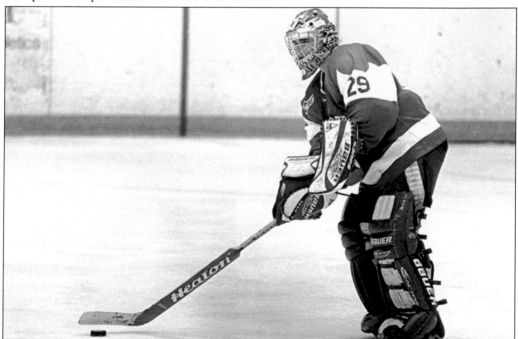

RICK DIPIETRO. The arrival of Rick DiPietro as Terrier net-minder for the 1999–2000 season created great excitement. The freshman goalie picked up where Larocque left off the previous February, with an outstanding goaltending performance in the Terriers' 4-1 victory over Boston College. DiPietro completed the double play, receiving Eberly and MVP awards in his only Beanpot appearance.